MEMOIRS OF A MARAUDER PILOT

F. William Bauers, Jr.

Edgewood Publishing Company

MEMOIRS OF A MARAUDER PILOT (c)
Copyright 2002 By F. William Bauers, Jr.

Published by Edgewood Publishing Company

All rights reserved. No part of this book may be reproduced or transmitted in any form or by any means, electronic or mechanical, including photocopying, recording, or by any information storage and retrieval system, without permission in writing from the publisher.

    First Printing: 2002
    Edgewood Publishing Company
    3201 New Mexico Ave, Suite 350
    Washington, D.C. 20016

    ISBN 0-9660611-2-8

Library of Congress Control Number: 2001132175
Printed in the United States of America

THIS BOOK IS DEDICATED TO THE

PILOTS AND CREWS OF THE

344th BOMBARDMENT GROUP

WHO GAVE THEIR LIVES

FOR OUR COUNTRY

AND TO MY WIFE, JOANNE TURNEY BAUERS,

AND OUR CHILDREN

CHRIS LORAN HILLS AND JONI CURRIER,

WHO SHARED THE POSTWAR JOURNEY

This was a press picture that I sent to my mother from Britain with a note on the back of the photo:

"I have a brand-new airplane, but this is Chuck Hardy's. The light was better. Hope you like it."

ACKNOWLEDGMENTS

This is to recognize with appreciation and gratitude the professionals, friends and family who assisted me, those who reviewed, formatted and edited the manuscript and those who made other substantive contributions.

Major General John O. Moench, USAF (Ret)
B-26 Pilot, Author, Historian

J.K. Havener, B-26 Pilot, Author

Lambert Austin, Author

Tom Brokaw, NBC, Author of *The Greatest Generation*

Joanne Turney Bauers, Cover Art

C. Loran Hills, Editor

Joni L. Currier, Software Engineer, Formatting

Professor J. Yuresha, Author, Producer, ABT

Thomas Owen, Cover Design & Layout

Robert Klenck, Author, Retired Minister, United Methodist Church

Sidney Kay, Actor and Drama Coach

BE NOT AFRAID OF LIFE

BELIEVE THAT LIFE IS WORTH LIVING

AND YOUR BELIEF

WILL HELP CREATE THE FACT

William James

FOREWORD

In the atmosphere of World War II, young men and women grew up fast. While a few did not adapt to the demands of military life, the majority not only did but also benefited therefrom. When the dust of war settled and these many individuals went back to what was viewed as more normal living, they carried forward with understanding and appreciation that was to shape their entire future life.

Those individuals who served with the B-26 Marauder units in World War II were both blessed and not-so-blessed. For political and other reasons, the Martin B-26 Marauder was the "dog" of the USAAF - later the USAF. In combat, the B-26 not only did an outstanding job but its losses were among the lowest of all heavy and other bomber aircraft flown. Nonetheless, the story of the B-26 Marauder and that of the men and women who were associated with this aircraft was not to be told until much later: During the time of World War II, the media generally relegated the exploits of the Marauder to a closing sentence reading "They also flew."

With no fanfare, the B-26 Marauder disappeared from the scene at the end of World War II. To confuse history in the years that followed, shortly after the end of World War II, the A-26 Invader was retitled the B-26 Invader with the result that the exploits of one B-26 often became the exploits of the other B-26.

With World War II over, the Marauder men and women sought to step away from the years of conflict, rising from the devastation of war and from years spent in learning things that had no direct application to the new world they were entering. A few members of this community went on to military careers, but most reentered the civilian community: Many obtained or completed the education that had been set aside during the war years. The ensuing heights achieved by these individuals is remarkable. While not recognized at the time, war did impart to all who were involved a strength and resolve that might not otherwise have been obtained and, as time went on, the nation and the world benefited.

Eventually, the Marauder community, individually and collectively, began to reflect on what had transpired during their lifetime. The individual and group conclusion was that the Marauder story was worth recording and, step by step, those who were a part of this story undertook to preserve the history of this great community. Progressively, this community reestablished bonds by way of association keyed to that of the individual wartime units and, finally, by way of an overall organization: The B-26 Marauder Historical Society.

Today the world is blessed with an array of B-26 Marauder writings, artworks and more. The story of the Marauder community, like the legendary phoenix of history, has literally risen from the ashes, with authors far and wide contributing their stories and their research to form an impressive body of knowledge. Few of these authors are what one would call professional writers. But all of them, motivated by the same drive that brought to the Allies the victory in World War II, have in their own special way added immeasurably to the record of the Marauder community.

This commendable work by F. William Bauers, Jr., adds one more interesting element to the Marauder story — a story that all but disappeared at the time, as in fact did all but a handful of the gallant airframes of the Martin B-26 Marauder.

> Major General John O. Moench, USAF (Ret)
> Historian, B-26 Marauder Historical Society

MEMOIRS OF A MARAUDER PILOT

CONTENTS

Preface		1
One	Throttles Forward	3
Two	The Early Years The Philippine Islands and Denver	11
Three	San Antonio and Fort Sam Houston	19
Four	Beginning a Military Career	39
Five	Training for War	57
Six	En Route to War	65
Seven	Based in Britain	81
Eight	Life in the U.K.	91
Nine	Combat Flying	99
Ten	On the Continent	129
Eleven	Washington, D.C.	151
Twelve	The Auditor General	173
Thirteen	Attaché Duty-Pakistan	183
Fourteen	The Strategic Intelligence School	211
Appendix		227

PREFACE

The name Marauder came from the British Royal Air Force (RAF), which flew some of the early production-line aircraft. The name they gave the aircraft was adopted by the U.S. Army Air Force (USAAF).

The emergency instructions in the operating manual for the Martin twin engine bombardment aircraft, the B-26 Marauder, included a classic understatement. It was roughly as follows: "Probably the most serious emergency which can arise is the failure of one or both engines on takeoff." It was unfortunately true. The B-26 Marauder had various names by which it was called, such as "the widow maker," "the flying prostitute" (no visible means of support) and "the flying coffin."

These sobriquets were a result of the short wingspan of the B-26. Because of the resultant reduction of lift, the aircraft took off and landed at a higher speed than other bomber aircraft. It was more dangerous to fly, especially for inexperienced pilots in transition training. Many crashed on takeoff, leading to the slogan "One a day in Tampa Bay." Tampa, Florida, was a principal location for transition training and supposedly the name lent itself to a slogan better than "Barksdale," a Louisiana training base. The B-26 Marauder developed a very bad reputation and came close to being scrapped by the Army. It was saved and proved itself worthy in combat. It took a lot of punishment and survived to return to base despite major damage. The B-26 was used successfully by the 9th Air Force in Western Europe flying combat missions at medium altitude against targets in France, Belgium and Germany, but it did not get the publicity that the "B-17s" of the 8th Air Force received and is not as well known.

The cockpit of a B-26 Marauder aircraft that flew many combat missions, "Flak Bait," is on display at the Smithsonian in Washington, D.C., in the aerospace museum. Because I had occupied a similar cockpit while flying 68 combat missions, my visit to the museum and seeing the remnant of this remarkable aircraft brought back fond memories, but also sadness. Life moves on.

Tom Brokaw's books *The Greatest Generation* and *The Greatest Generation Speaks* and his comments inspired me to write my story. Encouragement came from our daughters and from Sidney Kay, a member of the Rotary Club of Swarthmore, Pennsylvania. Lunchtime conversations with Sidney sometimes touched on important aspects of our lives. He had studied with the greats of the acting world at The Playhouse and at the Actors Studio in New York and was an actor and drama coach. His opinion was that the drama of my life, especially as a combat pilot in World War II, should be related to those who will never have the opportunity for similar experience.

It was a memorable time and an important era. My career spanned the development from the Army Air Corps to the U.S. Air Force, the period from Pearl Harbor to the end of World War II in Europe. Postwar service included assignments to Washington and as assistant air attaché to Pakistan following the partition of India. After leaving the service, I had the excitement of working in New York City and Washington, and internationally in particular in Spain and Mexico.

These pages cover my service in the USAF and its predecessors and the impact of the B-26 Marauder in WWII.

CHAPTER ONE

THROTTLES FORWARD

Takeoff

My concentration, as a combat pilot, was intense when taxiing onto the airfield runway for takeoff, thrusting the throttles of the B-26 Marauder forward, feeling the surge of power as the Pratt-Whitney engines revved up to takeoff RPM, and letting the plane roll. Excitement built as the aircraft sped down the runway for takeoff carrying a full crew and a bomb load of 4,000 pounds, lifting into the air to join 35 other B-26's in formation en route to a target on the continent of Western Europe.

For the pilot who had an engine failure on takeoff, pushing the throttles forward was almost his last act before the plane crashed and burned. Other pilots and crews were killed in midair collisions as they attempted to join formation in the darkness, the fog, or rain, all conditions of restricted visibility. Fortunately for me, I had a guardian angel and the aircraft engines always functioned well on take off. Not all were so fortunate.

One day, a friend, Warren Lonergan, a flight surgeon, asked me to accompany him from our base at Stansted, England, to pick up the remains of a pilot who had crashed a few miles from the base. I didn't think about it before responding and agreeing to go. We saw whoever was in charge of the situation, and Warren was handed a small bag containing the remains of what had been a pilot, an officer in what was then the Army Air Force. It was not possible for me to react at the time. I didn't know how. It was a shock as it was my first experience of that kind. I couldn't react personally because I didn't know the man, but it was the essence of tragedy. It made me feel terrible. I've never forgotten the incident.

There were other experiences equally tragic and more personal. All would be well and then antiaircraft fire, or flak, would start exploding around us. I watched friends being shot down, burning to death in the air after their plane received a direct hit, or crashing on landing in a badly damaged aircraft.

All was not bleak. There were good times at the pubs in Bishops Stortford and great times on trips to London and later to Paris. I enjoyed my close friendships with other pilots and crew members, felt the excitement of wartime and was gratified by my participation in the war. I believed that we were doing something important for our country. After flying 68 combat missions in the European Theater with the Ninth Air Force, I returned to the United States on July 4, 1945, fully expecting to be sent to the Pacific. However, the war ended after President Truman ordered the atomic bomb to be dropped on Hiroshima and Nagasaki, in August 1945.

I never had the desire to talk about the war after it ended; it was something to forget. But it wasn't possible to forget because it was deeply imbedded in my mind. While I went on to live a very interesting and happy life, I repressed the emotions that I felt and carried a deep underlying sadness as a result of my experience. Putting my story on paper has helped me to face the situations that I encountered, briefly relive them and put them behind me. While doing so I had nightmares for the first time, but now I feel that a weight has been lifted from my shoulders.

It is difficult to feel or to understand something one has never experienced. Many people had not been born at the time of World War II, or they were very young. Those living in the United States during the war experienced it from a different perspective. My goal is to contribute to an understanding of what occurred. Ultimately I reached a point where it was important for me to relate what it was like to be a B-26 Marauder bomber pilot, to fight a war in the air and to survive. As many others did not survive, I want this also to be their story of service in World War II.

After spending time in the U.S. Air Force following the war I went on to another career. Overall my life has been marvelous with a great deal of excitement, but there have been disappointments. The important thing is to have a goal and to persevere.

The combat incidents described are as clear and vivid now as when I lived them. They were the most dramatic or traumatic events in my life. Although we were not permitted to keep a diary or journal, I remember how it felt, and the faces of my friends.

I have endeavored to relate what my life was like growing up as an Army brat living on a military installation, going through flight training, flying a combat tour, facing danger, facing death. After the war I stayed in service as an Air Force officer for a while. I served in the United States, and then as an assistant air attaché in Pakistan, returning to Washington, D.C. After deciding to leave the Air Force I had an equally interesting career in business.

What has evolved is my philosophy. Many aspects of one's life can be controlled but others are subject to fate, to luck, to chance, and most important, to God's direction. Anyone you meet can influence your life, and certainly some friends had an impact on my life, influencing career choices and employment, and several times making the difference between life and death. It is possible to survive almost anything if you have courage, if your attitude is right, and you have a belief system in place. As my father advised me, if one door closes, another door opens. I have fought against certain changes, but they occurred. If you go with the flow, you may realize that the change was for the better. A balance between the mental, physical and spiritual aspects of life is important. Careers can be changed. It isn't necessary to stay in a field just because you once selected it. Intelligence, education, training and an open mind can propel you in a different direction. Enjoy your life; it is the only one you'll have.

This life offers choices, and although we are given different gifts, each of us has an obligation to make the most of what has been given. To obtain what we want, we have to determine what it is, visualize it, prepare as necessary to get it and then go for it without letting obstacles stand in the way, throttles forward. My becoming a pilot resulted from the desire, seizing the opportunity when it came and pursuing the goal; it required training, studying and acquiring the skills. At that time I could not anticipate where wearing the coveted silver wings would take me.

The B-26 Marauder played a major role in my life and in the life of other pilots who flew them, those who went to war in them and those who died in them. Medium bombers took part in the war in Africa, the Middle East, Italy, the Far East and Western Europe. In Europe the B-26 was involved in the war prior to, during and after the invasion, but this is not a history of either World War II or the B-26. It is my story as it relates to the Marauder.

My hope is to create a better appreciation of the B-26 Marauder aircraft, which initially had a bad reputation but became an important player before being scrapped at the end of WWII. I want to pay tribute to those who made the ultimate sacrifice, those whose lives were abruptly ended. They were intelligent, dedicated and capable. Some I knew only a short time, but the friendships were deep and it hurt when they were killed. Accepting the death of someone who is young and vital is difficult. Nevertheless, it was necessary to do so and go on. These pilots loved life and lived it well, but were willing to risk it all.

All the world's a stage
And all the men and women merely players
They have their exits and their entrances
And one man in his time plays many parts
(Shakespeare, *As You Like It*, Act II, Sc 7)

My entrance was in San Antonio, Texas.

CHAPTER TWO

THE EARLY YEARS

San Antonio

San Antonio, Texas, is the home of the Alamo, where a famous battle occurred in 1836 in the fight for Texas independence. It has long been a military center. Fort Sam Houston, a major army installation, is located there. The area also has become the home of major Air Force installations. At one time Randolph Field, now Randolph Air Force Base, located 17 miles northeast of San Antonio off the Austin Highway, was the principal location for Army Air Corps pilot training. Brooks Field, Kelly Field and Lackland, engineering, maintenance and training fields, were also located in the San Antonio area. Thus San Antonio was an appropriate and logical place for a future pilot in the U.S. Air Force to begin life. At the time I came onstage my parents did not contemplate my flying combat over Europe, or even becoming a pilot. My father's ambition was to have a son attend the U.S. Military Academy at West Point, and that became my goal.

My father was in the U.S. Army stationed at Fort Sam Houston, where he was to spend a large part of his Army career. Born in Austria, he left home in his early teens. After living in Vienna and Amsterdam he worked aboard transatlantic ships traveling between the United States and Western Europe. The United States became an irresistible lure. For a while he lived in New York City, then enlisted in the U.S. Army serving in Texas on the Mexican border, where he was a first sergeant with a cavalry troop, engaged in border warfare. In Eagle Pass, Texas, a border town, he met and married my mother. During World War I he received a commission as a second lieutenant and remained on active duty for 36 years, retiring as a lieutenant colonel.

Pop, as he was called by his family, loved the USA, the Army and horses. He rode all his life and after retiring had two horses. My parents' home at the time was across the street from a mansion owned by Mrs. Donald McNay. On her death it was left to the city for use as the San Antonio Museum of Art, including her own great collection of modern art. The estate had 60 acres of ground, and Mrs. McNay let Pop use the property as his own, to stable the horses there and to blaze riding trails.

To my father honesty and integrity were the two most important character traits. He believed that whatever you do should be done to the best of your ability. He also believed that any desired goal can be reached if your desire is strong enough and you work toward that goal. He was independent and self-contained, sometimes stern and demanding. A true patriot, he studied and read a great deal and had an excellent knowledge of history and of U.S. presidents.

When I was born, my parents were living in a small house on Drexel Avenue in San Antonio with my sister, Dorothy, who was two and a half. When I was almost two, my father was transferred to Manila, the Philippine Islands for station. We traveled from San Francisco on an Army transport ship, one of a fleet operated by the Army Transport Service, which has since been eliminated.

The Philippine Islands

In Manila, my parents had several servants, one of whom was my nanny. According to my mother, I became very attached to the nanny and didn't want to leave Manila without her when we sailed for the United States after the two-year tour was over. My sister was also looked after by the nanny but didn't have a similar attachment. Unfortunately I have no memory of my life in the tropics except what was related to me by my mother. My life wasn't too interesting, but my parents enjoyed theirs. They had an active social life with occasional invitations to dinner on some of the U.S. and foreign ships that came to Manila. They met foreign officers and dignitaries, including the Queen of Romania. Exotic foods from other countries served in the splendor of the captain's mess provided a pleasant break from their routine.

The Oriental Experience

On our return voyage to the United States the Army Transport ship put into port in China and Japan. At least I can say that I've been to those Far Eastern countries. I've always regretted that I don't remember anything about either the trip or the countries we visited. My mother bought a pair of Satsuma vases and some other oriental objets d'art that I always admired and that were left to me. Many Army families who were stationed in the Orient brought back Chinese rugs and oriental furnishings, which helped them create very interesting and beautiful homes, or "quarters," as they were called on Army posts. As a result of this exposure, things oriental have always seemed beautiful and exotic to me and led to our acquisition of Chinese and Persian rugs, Chinese chests and screens and art objects.

Denver

My first clear memory is of Denver, Colorado, when I was about four. Shortly after our arrival in Denver I was riding with my mother in the family's new black Buick Touring Sedan while she looked for a house to rent. As we drove up the driveway of a house on Race Street, my mother told me that previously the house had been occupied by gangsters. This was dramatic and scary information. Probably that is why I remember it. We did not rent the house! Instead my father was assigned quarters on the grounds of Fitzsimmons General Hospital, where he was stationed.

A Mountain Peak

On weekends the family would take automobile trips up into the mountains near Denver. The narrow roads were only one car width. When encountering a car coming from the other direction, one of the vehicles would have to back up to a wide spot in the road designed to allow passing. These spaces were far apart, leading to some hair-raising experiences. There were no guard rails, and I remember sitting in the backseat, looking out the window, down the side of the mountain to the valley, which seemed miles below, while the car was backing up. I was petrified then and I'm still uncomfortable driving in the mountains. Going up the mountain, it was easier to see an oncoming vehicle from the right front passenger seat than from the driver's seat. My mother, therefore, was designated to advise father if she saw a car coming down the mountain. When she saw one and screamed, Pop almost drove off the road. We made several trips to Pikes Peak to a miniature village that had a railroad. I always liked seeing the little buildings and trains. The visit was enjoyable once we were there, but not the trip.

Mahjong

Not much of this early period remains in my mind other than starting school and seeing tarantulas in our backyard. I remember visits to my parents' friends who lived in a very large house. After dinner, my sister and I would be sent upstairs to go to sleep while the adults played bridge or mahjong. Mahjong was a game brought back from the Orient. How the game was played was beyond my understanding, but I thought it was fascinating. The pieces in the mahjong set, somewhat similar to dominoes in size and shape, were made of ivory with oriental markings and mahogany backing. Playing the game consisted of drawing the pieces and discarding them until one player with the right combination won. My knowledge of the game was zero, but I liked the look and feel of the mahjong pieces.

Summer Camping Trips

During summer vacations we would drive from Denver to San Antonio to visit. My father liked nothing more than the outdoors and camping out. He had an umbrella tent with screen windows and doors, folding cots and chairs, a kerosene stove for cooking, and canvas buckets for washing hands and face. At night we would find a campground and Dad would pitch the tent, which had a center pole and four corner poles and steel stakes to hold the tent in place. My mother hated camping, but my sister and I thought it was fun. We always expected wild animals to come out of the surrounding darkness to devour us during the night, but that never happened. The camping experience was helpful later when I was in the Army, although in the Army we didn't have the same luxuries.

CHAPTER THREE

SAN ANTONIO AND FORT SAM HOUSTON

Return to San Antonio

After three years in Denver, when I was six or seven, we moved back to San Antonio. Dad was stationed at Fort Sam Houston, Texas, adjacent to San Antonio. My parents bought a house on Peck Avenue, on the south side of town. It was a charming house with brown stained shingles, a large lot and a double garage with servants quarters above. Because we didn't have servants my sister and I used the space above the garage for a playroom which was great for us. The house had a large living room with a fireplace. The master bath had a dressing room with built-in cabinets and drawers that pleased my mother. We all liked the house but didn't get to live there very long. Dad was assigned quarters at Fort Sam Houston, and lost his rental allowance, so the house had to be sold and we had to move.

Years later, on a return trip to San Antonio, I drove to Peck Ave to see the house but it had been destroyed to provide space for a freeway. I felt that a part of my past also had been destroyed.

Life at Fort Sam Houston

At Fort Sam Houston our quarters were in a row of large two-story buildings, each joined to other identical buildings by a covered walkway. Large steam pipes traversed the walkway and provided heat from a central steam plant. These buildings had comprised the wards of a hospital built during World War I. The hospital activity had been transferred to a new hospital building and the old buildings were converted to living accommodations for officers. Our quarters were one half of one of the buildings, ten large rooms on two floors.

The buildings were of frame construction, old and, as I discovered, flammable. One early evening a home across from us and just down the street caught fire and quickly burned to the ground. My memory is still vivid of the family's trying initially to get some of their belongings out of the house and then watching with horror as the building collapsed into burning embers despite the efforts of the fire department. The flames extended far above the building, lighting the night sky. After that incident I was fearful that the same thing might happen to our house but fortunately it did not.

Something worse happened to the family who occupied the other half of our building. Their teenage son, who was on a double date, was killed in an auto accident along with the beautiful daughter of another family who were friends of ours. They were thrown from the vehicle. I was eight at the time and still recall these tragic incidents.

Three Schools in Three Years

Because I had moved to Fort Sam Houston, I had to change schools for the third time. I was in the third grade. I did not feel good about walking into this school for the first time. I was ill at ease and had difficulty getting adjusted. The school authorities decided that I should skip a half grade, which added to the difficulty. But I adjusted and was elected president of the fifth-grade class. I remember being introduced as "El Presidente" and I liked the sound of it. In third grade I had my first crush on a redhead named Edna O'Hare. My best friend, Harold Gilbert, also liked her, and we had an altercation in the school yard because of her, but we remained friends. Harold's family had a Pierce Arrow, a large, elegant, expensive automobile, and I loved riding in it. The company that produced the Pierce Arrow, sometimes referred to as the American Rolls Royce, went out of business during the Depression.

Hogwash

Harold and I often got together to do experiments with our chemistry sets. We dumped the results of one experiment in the garbage. The garbage from Fort Sam Houston, under a contract, was picked up by a local entrepreneur and used to feed the hogs at a nearby hog farm.

My mother learned a short time thereafter that some hogs had died of unexplained causes. We thought that probably our chemistry experiment was responsible.

My Little Brother

When I was eight, my brother, Robert Edmond, was born. It had been my desire to have a brother, but I hadn't really thought it through. Somehow I believed that my brother would be a playmate, but eight years was too much difference in age. I thought he was a generally obnoxious brat.

My mother employed a woman named Buelah to help care for Bob and to assist with the housework. Between the two, my mother and Buelah, Bob was a spoiled baby who through persistence and tantrums always got what he wanted. From the time he was two he wanted to follow me whenever I went out to play and I didn't want to be bothered with him. If I didn't take him along, he would start screaming and my mother would insist that I let him go with me. He was an irritant and not what I had expected in a brother.

Our house had a porch that extended along the front of the house and down the side. Bob would strew his toys all the way along the porch and then Mother would ask me to pick them up. I would say, "Let him pick them up. They're his toys." She would respond, "He's just a baby." I believed that if he was big enough to spread the toys out, he was big enough to pick them up. But I always lost the argument.

The Depression

The Depression began about a year after my brother was born. Although I don't believe there was a connection, there could have been. The Depression made a lasting impression on many of those who lived through the era, as I am sure it did on me.

In Europe there was uncertainty and Germany had a major problem with inflation. In the United States overconfidence, speculation and excessive purchases of stock on margin culminated in the Wall Street collapse of 1929. The panic began on October 24, with 13 million shares traded that day. October 29, 1929, was considered the worst day in financial history. Investors lost heavily, and many of those who traded on margin were wiped out financially.

Mass unemployment followed the financial collapse. Adding to these difficulties, the drought in the Midwest created what was called the dust bowl and caused the migration of many distraught people in their derelict cars to other locations. These people were pictured in the newspapers, and the pictures were distressing.

My family and I were indeed fortunate. The military services continued to be paid and we lived very well, relatively speaking. Although military pay was reduced fifteen percent, prices were low and the pay cut didn't have a profound impact, although certainly it was felt. My parents bought food to take to others who were having a difficult time.

Two events made the most lasting impression. My cousin Elsie and her husband Ed lost their home to foreclosure and Charles, a friend of my parents, committed suicide when the bank holding his life's savings went under. Charles and Laura were close friends of my parents. Laura was a lovely, beautiful woman who never was able to dress well or to live well because of Charles's frugality. They spent little and saved for years in order to take a cruise and to buy a beautiful home when Charles retired. Laura had resented the manner in which they lived, and when the bank collapsed, losing all their savings, having sacrificed so long for naught, she had had enough. She divorced Charles, and Charles killed himself.

Bob as Adult and Army Officer

Brother Bob improved as he grew up although he never learned to manage his life or his money. In my opinion, my parents allowed too much latitude in his behavior: he was allowed to spend money freely without any responsibilities. Pop was transferred to a post near Galveston while my mother and Bob remained in San Antonio. Bob didn't have Pop's supervision, which he needed. He knew how to needle Mother and drive her to distraction, bugging her until she let him do what he wanted.

Dad and Bob were simpatico. Bob liked to go deer and turkey hunting with Pop (which I didn't). They had similar interests. Bob fulfilled Dad's ambition by graduating from the U.S. Military Academy at West Point. Although I wasn't able to attend, I was happy that he could. During the time he was attending West Point I was stationed in Washington and attended most of the Army football games. Bob and I got along well then, but after he graduated from the academy we were always stationed in different parts of the country or overseas and didn't see each other often. While serving in Germany he persuaded Betty Middleton, whom he had dated while stationed in El Paso, to fly to Germany from El Paso and marry him. It was a good move on his part. We welcomed Betty into the family. She has an excellent sense of humor, which she needed while married to Bob.

Bob served twenty years in the U.S. Army. He worked in the missile field in the United States, and served in both Korea and Vietnam. These two combat tours had an adverse effect on him. He and Betty were divorced, and he had difficulty coping with life after that. He died at a relatively young age.

Mother

Mother was a sweet, compassionate and empathetic woman, who devoted her life to the care of her children, her mother and her husband. She had a good sense of humor and loved to read. Her library at the time of her death contained more than 2,000 books. My friends always liked her and enjoyed visiting our home. She was interested in people and was able to draw them out. In hospital waiting rooms she became a friend of whoever sat next to her.

Once she dialed a wrong number. The woman who answered said, "You interrupted me, I was just about to kill myself." Mother talked her out of suicide and became a phone pal, calling frequently.

I thought that Mother was pretty, as others did. When the family lived in Denver she often wore a coat with a fur collar and cuffs and a flattering hat. One day as we stopped at the entrance gate to Fitzsimmons the guard on duty told her that she was the best-looking woman in Denver. She lived off that compliment for years.

Mother liked to play bridge and dance but didn't have the opportunity very often to engage in either activity. My father worked hard at his job and his other interests were hunting, riding, golf and swimming. He also liked to work on his autos and in his workshop.

My Pioneer Grandmother

My maternal grandmother was from Zurich, Switzerland, born to a wealthy, influential and aristocratic family. She married against her parent's wishes. My grandfather was from Denmark, and was living in Hamburg where he owned a jewelry store. As he was not of the aristocracy and they considered him a Prussian, he was not acceptable to my grandmother's parents, and she was disinherited. My grandparents left Europe in the late 1800's and settled in Texas, on a farm near Eagle Pass. Farming was not their forte.

My grandfather died of a heart attack when I was about six months old. My grandmother came to live with my parents and continued to do so until her death many years later at the age of 94. Although she had a disability from polio, she traveled from Zurich to Texas with three children and had two more children while living in Texas.

She was uncomplaining about her situation and philosophical about life, spending hours in a rocking chair. Her attitude was that one should be content with one's situation. This remarkable woman gave up everything for love - a life of luxury, an inheritance, her family and her country. My grandmother, with a major disability, was a pioneer. As a result of polio, her right leg was shorter than the left. She wore a steel device that enabled her to walk. The device was heavy and uncomfortable. She also used a cane or a walking stick and always wore full-length skirts. My mother cared for her until her death.

Grandma played the piano, especially Chopin and Straus waltzes. I liked to sit on the piano bench and listen to her play. She was fluent in French and German, as well as English. I wish that she had taught me those two languages but I never asked her to do so and as a child didn't believe that I would ever go to Europe. It seemed very far away. She did teach me to play chess and we often played for hours. She gave me a copy of Rudyard Kipling's poem "If" and suggested that I live by it. My grandmother was a strong influence on me, and the only grandparent I knew.

It must have been painful for her to talk about her family as she never discussed them or her illustrious background. One of the few stories Grandma told me was of the time her family had to flee their home in Alsace-Loraine during the Franco-Prussian war. When they returned home there were bullet holes in the walls.

Her father, Dr. Carl Schinz, was involved in scientific activities on both sides of the Atlantic. My grandmother was born in Philadelphia but lived in Zurich in the family home, the Seidenhof, and in Strasbourg and Basel. A room from the Seidenhof, known for its ceramic stove and wood paneling from the fifteenth century, is in the national museum in Zurich, near the railroad station.

Another Move

The old hospital units that provided our home at Fort Sam Houston were scheduled for demolition to make room for new construction. Dad was assigned another set of quarters, a single family, brick building with plastered walls and a big porch along the front and side of the house. We preferred our new home to the previous quarters, although it was smaller.

A room from my great grandfather's home, The Seidenhof, now in the National Museum in Zurich. (the Schinz Room)

Life on an Army Post

A swimming pool and tennis courts were near our quarters, and that was a great advantage. During the summer much of my day was spent at the pool. Two boys close to my age lived on the block and we used to play cops and robbers and cowboys and Indians. We built a covered wagon and a tree house, but we had to take down the tree house due to its lack of esthetic qualities, as judged by the military authorities. The movie theater was nearby and the admission cost was low, so I was able to go to the movies almost every night. The balcony was reserved for officers and families (now not politically correct), and we usually sat on the front row of the balcony behind the railing for an unobstructed view.

Again there was a death next door. My friend Buddy, a wiry kid with red hair, had joined the Boy Scouts and went to a summer camp with the troop. While camping he developed appendicitis. Apparently it wasn't initially considered serious. Buddy's appendix had ruptured by the time he was brought back home. The medics were not able to save him. I didn't understand why he should die at his age (nine or ten). I thought it was because he had done something wrong and he was being punished. As a result of Buddy's death, my mother would not allow me to join the Boy Scouts, despite my many appeals.

A few years later, Buddy's father, Harry, died of a heart attack. Buddy's mother, who often chatted with my mother, would qualify every comment about their plans with " . . . when Harry retires . . . " They had bought a lot in Hollywood, Florida, and were going to build there, ". . . when Harry retires." They were going to buy a new car " . . . when Harry retires." They were going to travel . . .I decided that waiting until retirement to live your life was not a good idea. Besides, why retire?

At the nearby swimming pool, often there were fabulous cars parked in the lot. My favorite was a Cadillac V-16 Phaeton, which was so beautiful that I could just sit and look at it. A major general assigned to staff post had a long black Cadillac limousine and driver. There were other majestic and beautiful autos such as the Cord, Auburn and La Salle. At that stage I could identify on sight, by make and model, almost any car on the road. My father bought a Marquette, which was produced for only one year by General Motors. It was a distinctive car, but GM chose not to continue it. The next family car was a 1937 Oldsmobile, which had very advanced styling. While driving to pick up Pop from his office I had an accident at an intersection. I encountered a friend and had a conversation that made me late. In a hurry to get there, I failed to make a full stop at a stop sign. It was just a smashed fender, but I felt terrible about it and vowed never to drive again. Pop made me get in the other car right away and drive it. The Cavalry philosophy was that if you fall off your horse, get back on and ride.

Death of a Polo Player

During the pre-WWII era in which I grew up, an Army officer had social status, as in most other countries. Some officers were from wealthy families and others had married into wealth. There was social interchange with San Antonio society. All conduct was decorous, but a major scandal occurred when a polo player, a member of the Army polo team, an elite group, had an affair with a San Antonio socialite and was shot and killed. I don't remember whether the death was by the hand of the lady or her husband, but the incident made large headlines in San Antonio newspapers for days.

The First Career Decision

While growing up at Fort Sam Houston, I thought that living on an Army post was great. There were parades, ceremonies and band concerts. The facilities included swimming pools, tennis courts, a golf course and riding stables. There was always company with other kids around. As teenagers we could attend the dances or "hops" at the officers' club on Saturday nights. The military post was a protected environment where we never locked doors and felt safe. Not for the reasons above but when I was seven years old I decided that I wanted to be an Army officer and never wavered from that goal. I liked the sense of duty, of purpose, honor and integrity and service to the country.

Junior High

Hawthorne was the junior high school that I attended in San Antonio. I started driving at age 13, and when I was in the eighth grade I was allowed to drive a car to school. Other than that all I remember about junior high is a friend who was active in all school activities and a role model, and a favorite teacher who died suddenly. A week before she died, I had a dream in which she was in a casket. When she actually died it really shook me. I wondered if somehow I might have been the cause because I dreamed it before it happened. My teacher had a favorite song that the class was taught to sing and every time thereafter that I've heard the music I have thought of her. I still remember the music but not her name.

Along the way I learned that my dream was considered a "precognitive" dream. I've also had two others. Fascinating, but I don't understand the phenomena. I just know that having such a dream can be very disturbing.

First Date

At fourteen I attended the movies with Jane, the redhead next door, Buddy's sister. We went to the theater on the post. At that stage it was acceptable to go to the movies or to parties at the girls' homes or at the club. My first date was at age sixteen, a senior in high school. Also at sixteen I had my first real crush on a girl who lived on the post, also named Jane, who wasn't allowed to date. Thus we could only meet at parties and take walks.

High School

My first two years of high school I attended Thomas Jefferson High School across town in San Antonio, a beautiful new school. The Army brats from Fort Sam Houston were bused to and from school in old "liberty" trucks. These trucks with canvas tops had been converted into school busses by installing benches on either side of the truck and adding steps at the rear. The drivers considered us a raucous group. Some of the drivers liked to race along Hildebrand Avenue, a cross-town thoroughfare with some major hills. The trucks went really fast downhill! It is surprising that we were not all killed, but we loved the excitement and cheered the drivers on. I disliked being bused because I couldn't participate in any after-school activities and never felt part of the group, not being able to share activities outside of school.

As a freshman in high school at fourteen I joined the ROTC at Thomas Jefferson High and stayed in it for two years, drilling and carrying a rifle. As a result, my right shoulder is lower than my left. My goal was to be an officer in the ROTC in my third year, as a senior. My parents, however, decided to build a house in Alamo Heights, an incorporated city on the north side of San Antonio, as a permanent home. So we moved and it was necessary for me to transfer to Alamo Heights High School for my senior year. At both schools I took courses that I thought would help me gain entrance to West Point.

New Kid on the Block

Most of my classmates at Alamo Heights had lived in the community, gone to school together and known each other most of their lives. Coming in from the outside I again was not part of the group, but as someone new I had curiosity status. I developed some friendships and started dating different girls, among them the girl voted "most popular" and the girl voted the "cutest." I had a crush on the girl voted "most beautiful," but she was involved. Most of my fellow students were from well to do families who lived in Alamo Heights, Terrell Hills or Olmos Park, upscale suburbs of San Antonio. Many of the kids had their own cars and some came to school in chauffeur-driven sedans or limos. Some of the girls I knew had parties at their homes; most of the homes were beautiful; some of them were mansions. Many parties were given at the San Antonio Country Club. On summer evenings there were outdoor dances with an air of fantasy — the orchestra playing, music wafting across the terrace on the summer breezes, the lighting lending enchantment and dancing under the stars. These evenings were memorable. I liked the lifestyle my fellow students lived and wanted to emulate it.

An Interest in History

My history teacher at Alamo Heights, Lorraine Lighthouse, known as Teach, was an attractive redhead just out of college. My friend, K.L. Berry, a football player and son of an Army colonel, and I always sat in the front row in history class and paid rapt attention to Teach. We both got A's in history. Teach was active in student affairs and head of the Girl Reserves. She insisted that I learn to dance, attend the Girl Reserve dances and date a particular girl whom she thought suitable. I did learn to dance and got A's in history, even though I didn't learn much history and nothing clicked with the girl.

Don't Blame Joe Camel

When I started dating I also started smoking. Most of the girls smoked cigarettes. Thus I carried cigarettes in my shirt pocket. I tried smoking to appear more worldly; once I tried it, I was hooked and smoked for years, enough to cause respiratory problems and loss of lung capacity. After four tries and a physician's demand I finally managed to quit smoking.

Liquor was available at all the parties, even though most of us were sixteen or seventeen; my seventeenth birthday was ten days prior to graduation. None of us thought much about liquor's being available and I don't recall anyone in high school who drank too much. Liquor and beer were available at home, but my parents rarely drank. I didn't drink at home, other than a beer with Mexican food, although I was not restricted.

Prep School - a Short Prep

Following high-school graduation I attended a military prep school at Camp Bullis, Texas, to prepare for the entrance exams for the U. S. Military Academy at West Point. The prep school was difficult academically but I liked being away from home and liked the school. All was well until a medical officer from Fort Sam, who was on the examining board, told me that because of my allergies, I would not pass the West Point physical. At that time, allergies disqualified applicants for entry to the academy, and there were records of my treatment for allergies at Fort Sam Houston. Therefore, he said, I was wasting my time and that of the school. Based on his comments, my parents withdrew me from prep school.

What a devastating blow! Inasmuch as for most of my life I had planned for and anticipated attending West Point, I was demoralized. I did not have an alternative plan. I decided to get a job and work until I knew what I wanted. A summer-long discussion (argument) with my parents ensued. They insisted that I go to college and I didn't want to. We compromised on a local business college with a two-year course of study to prepare for the CPA exam. Because I wasn't truly motivated, my attendance was a relative waste of time. Nevertheless I did well and finished the course in minimum time. The San Antonio Public Service Company employed me in the Treasury Department.

Joining the Guard

At the age of eighteen I joined the Texas National Guard, Company A, 141st Infantry Regiment, 36th Division. My goal was to qualify to take the competitive exam for a National Guard appointment to West Point and take the physical exam in another location. Several Army brat friends also signed up: Stanley Kennedy, Bob Kendall and Curtis McComas. On Tuesdays we carpooled to the Armory for training. Usually we did too much kidding around at drill and wound up being called on by the first sergeant: "Bauers, Kennedy and Kendall, fall out and sweep the Armory." We didn't mind too much and thought that it gave us a certain status. It also brought me to the attention of the company commander. He called me into his office to tell me essentially that I had promise if I would shape up.

Summer Camp

The Texas National Guard was sent to Palacios, Texas for two weeks of summer camp, traveling by train from San Antonio. This was an exhilarating adventure for me. Shortly after arrival at the camp, the captain promoted me to corporal and squad leader. I was able to get my buddies who were Army brats, and who knew the ropes, assigned to the same squad — my squad. There was formal competition between the squads, scored on close-order drill, appearance of uniforms and rifles, marksmanship and other factors. My squad was selected as best in the company and the company was best in the division; I concluded that we were best in the division.

On the way home from camp, most of the troops on the train became ill from food poisoning. Our train was met by a chain of ambulances. It was a dramatic homecoming! I hadn't eaten the food because it didn't taste right, so I was helping everyone who was ill. We made the front pages of the newspapers with the troops hanging out of the train windows, being carried off the train on stretchers and off to the hospital in ambulances. It was an ignominious end to our summer encampment.

Before the Storm

In my late teens I felt more independent than I had ever felt before. Having no real responsibility, earning money, although not a large amount, and doing as I pleased was wonderful. Dating and going to parties, including the debuts of some of the girls I knew in high school, was fun. I had friends to hang out with, Jack Mingos and Tommy Reiner.

Jack was dark-haired and intense. At different times we had dated the same girl. Both of us got dumped so we had that in common. One night Jack and I went out to commiserate and we were drinking rum and coke. I got sick afterward and spent the night at Jack's home, going to my home the next morning in my white dinner jacket. I have never touched rum since. Unfortunately Jack was killed during WWII.

Tommy lived in Terrell Hills, had a convertible and liked to have a good time. An excellent diver, he spent a lot of time at the pool, diving from the high board. With good looks, a great physique, deep tan and white swimming trunks, he got a lot of attention from the young ladies. Hanging out with him enhanced my status. Tommy became a pilot in the Air

Force and we crossed paths in Waco, Texas, but then we lost touch.

Meanwhile in Europe

While I was in my teens, relatively unconcerned about the world's problems, the world was changing and not for the better. Much of Europe had been occupied by Germany or was threatened by Hitler. The unemployed in Europe had joined the bourgeoisie in following the Fascist National Socialist and Communist movements, which thrived on their despair. In 1933, Hitler sent German troops into the Rhineland, the district that had been demilitarized under the Treaty of Versailles. The Nazis seized Austria in March, 1938.

In an attempt to avert war, Britain's Prime Minister Chamberlain met with Hitler and was accused of appeasement. Britain announced that if France went to war over Czechoslovakia, Britain would stand by France. After Germany and Russia signed a nonaggression pact in August 1939, with Germany's eastern flank safe, Hitler attacked Poland on September 1. On September 3, 1939, Britain and France declared war against Germany.

CHAPTER FOUR

BEGINNING A MILITARY CAREER

Mobilization of the National Guard

World War II had begun, and it seemed likely that the United States would become involved. Germany had bombed Warsaw. In mid-September, German troops marched into Poland. The Russians began their invasion of Finland in November 1939 and bombed Helsinki. In May 1940 the Nazis invaded Holland, Belgium and Luxembourg by land and air and pierced the French Maginot Line on a 62-mile front. By May 22, the Nazis had reached the channel and trapped the British forces in Belgium, forcing their evacuation at Dunkerque. Italy declared war on Great Britain and France in June 1940, and the Germans occupied Paris.

Although President Roosevelt had declared United States neutrality, he had begun to rearm. It was apparent that the U.S. would enter the war but at that time we were not taking life too seriously. All was about to change.

In November 1940, the Texas National Guard (along with other state National Guard units) was mobilized and ordered to active duty at Camp Bowie. The camp, named after one of the heroes of the Alamo, was located at Brownwood, Texas, about 185 miles north of San Antonio. The contractors building the encampment were behind schedule, and the roads had not been completed. Because of unprecedented rain, the tent city was a quagmire.

Members of the Guard who were attending school were eligible for discharge, but I was more interested in leaving home and going on active duty than in going to school. Getting away seemed like an opportunity. Going on duty with a hometown unit, with friends, made for a relatively easy transition to the Army.

My promotion to sergeant came along quickly. I was a platoon sergeant with responsibility for 60 men. Army life seemed natural to me as I had grown up in it; I liked the military service and had friends among the other noncommissioned officers. For that stage, it was a good outdoor life.

While working in San Antonio I had saved enough money to buy a used 1938 Buick coupe, which made my life worthwhile. The car gave me mobility. If I were able to get a weekend pass I could drive to San Antonio. Often I would spend the weekend in San Antonio, drive back to camp late on Sunday night and then get up by dawn's early light to go on a 25-mile march on Monday, carrying a rifle and backpack. By nightfall I was able to sleep on a pile of rocks and often did. We marched, camped out and had practice on the rifle and pistol range along with other military training. I qualified as expert in both rifle and pistol and loved target practice.

On occasion I pushed the envelope, returning to Camp Bowie just in time to change clothes and fall out for roll call. Not going to bed was an advantage. As I wrote on a postcard, "At least I didn't have to make my bed this morning." Fortunately I could recuperate by sleeping Monday evening and night.

We were training for war and I also wanted to advance in rank, so life was not easy. In February 1940, I wrote home at 1:00 A.M. "If you wonder what I'm doing up at this hour of the night, I'm on guard. In fact, I'm Sergeant of the Guard. What a job! We got up at 4:15 this morning and were out on the range till after 7:00 P.M. I had to round up the guard detail, orderlies, runners and a truck to take them around. Now I have to stay up all night. I hope I get to sleep tomorrow. Thank God we finish firing Thursday."

In March 1940, I wrote to my father who was then stationed at Camp Wallace, Hitchcock, Texas, near Galveston. "Dear Dad, We went on a 12-mile hike this morning, had bayonet training and stood retreat this evening. So I don't feel like writing a letter. Just thought I'd let you know I got back okay."

Offsetting any hardship, the money was great! "Today is payday. I owed Bob $3.00, Loan $5.25, Show book $2, Laundry $1.35, Radio $10.50, Total is $22.50. I'm sending $35.00 home. Please make the radio payment and pay what other bills I owe. I figure I'll have $12.00 left for the rest of the month, which I believe will be enough. My pay was $59.20 because promotions didn't go into effect until February 5."

"Yesterday and today were fairly easy. However, it's not for long. Next week we start combat firing, and the combat range is 12 miles from camp. All available trucks have been sent to Oklahoma to move troops to Abilene, so–" That meant that we'd be walking. I continued training at Camp Bowie through August 1941. The division went on maneuvers in August but I didn't have to go because I had been selected to go to Fort Benning, in Columbus, Georgia. I wasn't sorry that I didn't go on maneuvers; been there, done that the year before. It was a strange feeling, nevertheless, when the division pulled out without me.

Commission as a Second Lieutenant

The 36th Division had administered an IQ test to the troops called an AGCT, or Army General Classification Test. My score was sixth highest in the division. As a result the company commander called me in and suggested that I apply for officer training at the Infantry School, Fort Benning. Qualifying for one of the slots, I was off to Fort Benning in my trusty Buick.

At Fort Benning I wrote a postcard: "This is a wonderful place. The instructors are excellent, brilliant and amusing, and the subjects very interesting. However, there certainly isn't any time to be spared. We get up at 5:30. Classes start at 7:30 and end at 5:05. Study hall from 7 to 9. Lights go out at 10." Another day, "I don't have time to write because we're going to have a test on the 37mm antitank gun and 50 caliber machine gun on Saturday, which I am trying to pass."

The curriculum included instruction on Weapons, Tactics, Communication, Automotive subjects, General subjects including Motor and Rail Movement, Care of Equipment, Company Administration and Mess Management, Hasty Field Fortification, Map and Aerial Photo Reading, and others. We were required to complete 529 hours of instruction in three months.

On December 12, 1941, I was commissioned as a Second lieutenant in the Army of the United States and allowed to pin on the single gold bars. I was an Army officer! My first career goal had been reached, although by a different route than the one originally planned. I was disappointed that my parents couldn't be there for the graduation ceremony, presided over by Brigadier General Omar Bradley, but the war had begun and Pop was well occupied with logistics at Camp Wallace. General Bradley was to become famous during World War II.

The Attack on Pearl Harbor

Five days earlier, on December 7, 1941 ("a date which will live in infamy," as President Franklin D. Roosevelt intoned in his radio address) I had attended church in Columbus, and a wonderful family with a young daughter invited me to lunch after church. The home was beautiful, the daughter was lovely and I was having a most enjoyable time. Suddenly a neighbor came running in, very animated, to ask if we had been listening to the radio, which of course we hadn't. She said that the Japanese had just bombed Pearl Harbor! My hosts turned on the radio immediately. We heard the announcement of this unbelievable event and the call for all Fort Benning personnel to return immediately to Fort Benning. That was the end of a beautiful day — and of an era.

San Antonio Rose

In San Antonio I had been dating a lovely girl from the time I was nineteen, and we were quite serious. As the old adage states, "The course of true love never runs smooth." Her father was a major general, commanding the Texas National Guard, and that was not a problem until I went on active duty with the National Guard as an enlisted man. She was advised by her father that she could no longer go out with me. That provided an additional incentive for me to get a commission so that it would be acceptable for us to date. As a commissioned officer, I could go out with her. While working toward that goal at Benning, I was incredibly busy, up at five thirty in the morning and occupied with training, drill, exercise or study every minute until taps at ten p.m. As a result, I didn't write and therefore got a "Dear John" letter. She married another, who she said reminded her of me. Inasmuch as the war had begun and everything was uncertain, it was my feeling that it was not the time to marry. But I thought the situation was ironic.

Christmas at Fort Jackson, South Carolina

Following my graduation from Fort Benning Officer Candidate School, OCS, my first official orders directed me to Fort Jackson in Columbia, South Carolina. After a short leave in San Antonio, I hit the road in the Buick just before Christmas, 1941, and reported in at 30th Division Headquarters, Fort Jackson. A hotel room in Columbia was my temporary residence as there were no officers' quarters available at Fort Jackson. I spent Christmas Eve and

Christmas Day in my hotel room drinking bourbon and feeling very much alone and miserable. It was my first Christmas away from home.

A Home Away From Home

After Christmas an officer from Fort Jackson was showing me around Columbia, and we passed a very beautiful home. I commented on the attractiveness of the architecture and the setting. By coincidence he was acquainted with the owners, who had been renting a room as a contribution to the war effort. He made the introduction and I gained a beautiful room — but it was much more than that. The Hartleys treated me as a member of the family and continually invited me for meals until I felt ill at ease accepting. But Mrs. Hartley was insistent, and it was hard to refuse. They were charming people. As they owned a wholesale grocery chain and the hostess was a remarkable cook, the food was always delicious. To add to the equation, they had a beautiful daughter. Annabelle was engaged to an Air Force captain, a pilot, and I was too honorable, or too stupid, to pursue her. They were married and unfortunately during the war he was killed in action.

Mrs. Hartley introduced me to a beautiful young lady who was chosen Queen of the University of South Carolina and was a candidate in the Miss South Carolina contest. One night I invited her to go to a movie at Fort Jackson, which was an error in judgment. The lights were still on when we entered the theater and it was filled with soldiers. A near riot ensued when she walked down the aisle, with a lot of whooping, hollering and stomping feet.

The Tank Destroyer

My initial assignment at Fort Jackson with the 30th Division was with an infantry company, and later with a tank-destroyer unit. Tank destroyers were a new concept: they were basically tanks built with the armament to destroy other tanks. At that stage we had neither proper military equipment nor operating procedure. Small half-ton trucks played the part of tank destroyers and brooms served as antitank guns, literally! It reminded me of the days when I was nine years old and converting household items into imaginary weapons.

The 30th Division principally was made up of National Guard units from North and South Carolina and Georgia, a good group of men. I was a platoon commander and also conducted basic training for recruits. I liked what I was doing, and although I enjoyed it, my concern was that I might be retained in the United States as an instructor, whereas I wanted involvement in the war that was now active in North Africa.

From Fort Jackson our unit was transferred to Fort Hood, at Killeen, Texas; Killeen became the Army's tank destroyer headquarters. While in South Carolina, like most Texans, I had bragged too much about Texas. As most of the troops did not like Fort Hood (a gross understatement) I took a lot of good-natured abuse. Fort Hood was in Texas, however, much closer to San Antonio than Fort Jackson, and I could visit home. It didn't matter what anyone said about Texas.

Silver Wings

At that point in my life I did not have a college degree, which had been a prerequisite for Army pilot training. As a teenager in San Antonio I had envied the young pilots who breezed into San Antonio in their convertibles, wearing their uniforms and silver wings, dating and sometimes marrying the most attractive young ladies, including my sister. Furthermore, I had become tired of walking and eating dust and dirt as an infantry man. The war in North Africa provided newspaper pictures of burning tanks with the crews trapped inside. Flying seemed infinitely more appealing.

While growing up I always had felt uncomfortable looking down from heights, probably a result of my mountain experiences as a kid in Colorado. I had never flown but it was from lack of opportunity, not fear. After I went on active duty with the Army, my sister's husband, who was a pilot, took me up for my first flight. I liked flying! The feeling in a plane was quite different from what it was from a stationary height like a mountain or a building. I didn't have a problem with it.

The Army Air Corps opened pilot training to any qualified commissioned officer and I decided to apply. The battalion commander, who thought I had potential in the Army and who had promoted me to first lieutenant, refused to submit my application for pilot training. I had to wait until he was away and then persuade the battalion executive officer to forward my application. The exec had been manager of the Memphis Airport and was understanding of my desire to fly. On his return to Fort Hood, the commander told me that I was making a big mistake, but I pursued the application.

The physical exam at Randolph Field lasted several days and included aptitude tests using mechanical devices to determine response, coordination and manual dexterity. My manual dexterity was not great, which was an advantage as I was selected for pilot training rather than bombardier. My eyes were 20/15 and my hearing was excellent. My orders to flight school, with preflight in San Antonio, were soon received; this was the icing on the cake. I entered pilot training in the Class of 43-I.

PreFlight

In preflight at Lackland Army Air Field in San Antonio, there was much to learn. As I recall, we studied the theory of flight, aerodynamics, aircraft identification, engines, navigation, meteorology and other related aspects. The training course at Lackland on the south side of San Antonio lasted nine weeks. Most of the day was spent in class and I never liked sitting in class. What was great was the emphasis on physical conditioning. Every morning we ran for three miles. Running was invigorating and I've never felt better. At that stage I could eat anything that I wanted and not gain weight. So I had ice cream for dessert at breakfast, lunch and dinner. Upon completion of preflight we were assigned to primary flying school. My assignment was Cuero, Texas.

Primary Flight Training

Cuero was a small town of 5,000 people. The air base was a civilian airfield that had been converted to military flight training. As there were no quarters at the field, the student officers had to find a place to live, which is sometimes difficult in a small town. Two other student officers, Al Catlin and Johnny Bowden, and I found a big old house that had been vacant for twenty years; it belonged to an estate. To this day I believe that the house was haunted. There was a skeleton in one of the closets — a real skeleton — and a secret stairway with access through a sliding wall panel. The main stairway had a large landing and a big window over the landing. The furnishings were in keeping with the house — old. In the living room there was a windup Victrola and two records. One of the records was, "Jeanine, I Dream of You in Lilac Time." I don't remember what the other record was. We preferred the radio, but then we weren't at home very often. One night I was home alone during a thunderstorm. The lightning ominously lit up the large window over the landing and the rain was coming in around the window. Then the lights in the house went off. There were strange noises; it was the classic haunted house. I went outside and stood in the rain.

My Primary Instructor

In primary flight school, each aspiring pilot was assigned to an instructor, the majority of whom were civilian pilots with Brayton Flying Service, under contract to the U.S. government. My instructor was a small wiry man with a nasty attitude and a vicious temper. He had "washed out" or eliminated all of his students in the previous class and was endeavoring to do the same with my class. He had seven students assigned to him. For our initial flight instruction we were scheduled to have eight hours of instruction in the Fairchild PT-19 A and then solo. There was strong pressure on the students to solo and strong competition to solo first. I was a bit slow to get the hang of it. Eight hours passed, then nine hours, and I was concerned. After ten hours my instructor said that he was going to sit on the bench and have a cigarette and told me to take the plane around. I was thrilled! After takeoff, when up in the air, I realized that I was going to have to get the plane back down on the ground on my own for the first time. I made a good approach and a beautiful landing and taxied back to the flight line. The instructor said nothing except, "Take it around again."

Student officers were treated the same as the cadets, and that was fine with me. In this case we took more abuse. The PT-19 A was an open-cockpit aircraft with dual seats, front and rear, controlled by a stick and rudder. The stick was on the floor of the cockpit in the center extending up between the knees, and there were dual controls front and rear. The student sat in front and the instructor in the rear, or vice versa. Some instructors used the stick as a club. The instructor could without warning shake the stick violently from side to side, which would bang the knees of the student in the other cockpit. My knees were black and blue. In addition I suffered severe verbal abuse in the form of profane insults. Other students were enduring the same, and we thought it must be part of the course.

I learned, however, that my instructor was unhappy in the job. He wanted to break his employment contract in order to become a test pilot. He believed that if he continued to wash out all his students his employment would be terminated. Thus he was treating his students unfairly.

When I taxied in after my first solo and beautiful landing, I expected at least a minor compliment or congratulations. When my instructor said nothing, it offended me and I was thinking about his attitude when I went back up instead of what I was doing. My speed was excessive when I landed the second time. The plane bounced a couple of times and then veered toward the fence. I was able to brake before hitting the fence and there was no damage other than to my ego. This time, though, when I taxied in I really was hit with everything he had, including the threat of being washed out.

Ripper

In primary flight training at Cuero I developed a new nickname. As student pilots we were assigned parachutes that had seat packs. The chute strapped on your back and you sat on the seat pack while in the cockpit. We wore the chutes both on the flight line and in the aircraft. The students were scheduled for an hour of flight instruction with the instructor on a rotating basis; he would taxi in, one student would get out and another would climb aboard. The instructor did *not* like to be kept waiting. One day as I was rushing to get out to the plane, I hiked up the seat pack and inadvertently opened the chute. Yards of white silk trailed out behind me across the flight line. It was one of life's really embarrassing moments. After this event my fellow students dubbed me Ripper.

Aerobatics and the 40-Hour Check

Flight training continued and gradually as student pilots we had less dual time with the instructor and more solo time. We learned to do slow rolls, snap rolls, and spins — aerobatics. I loved aerobatics and felt totally free. When I flew solo it seemed that everything went well, but with the instructor in the rear cockpit I never did anything right, at least not according to him. He always made me angry and I objected to his insults and profanity, but I couldn't say anything. By this time I had almost 40 hours of flying time. I believe I was one of three students left out of his original seven. I had my 40-hour check by a military pilot who was known for being tough and that check was make-or-break time. If you failed the forty-hour check you were out. I passed easily.

Up for Elimination

My instructor's comment was, "I don't know how you did it!" After about five more hours of flight time my instructor became really angry one day and put me up for elimination. This was a crushing blow. I was determined to become a pilot, loved flying and was doing the best I could do. At that time being put up for elimination by your primary-flight instructor was tantamount to the end of your military flying career. I went out that night and got loaded because I thought my flying days were over.

The next morning I was scheduled for my elimination ride with a military check pilot and I was totally relaxed. What I did wouldn't matter. By the luck of the draw, the same tough military pilot who had given me my forty-hour check was assigned for the elimination ride. Before we took off, he said, "What's the matter? I just rode with you and it wasn't a bad ride." Coming from him that was a supreme compliment. Since he had asked, I told him of my problems with my instructor and of my trouble flying with him in the plane. He said, "Well, you have to learn to fly under pressure." We took off and he told me to do a few maneuvers; in my relaxed state, I did them well. He said, "Let me show you how to do a loop." At that point I knew I was home free. After landing, he said, "I'm going to assign you to another instructor." That was thrilling to hear and it was a very rare accomplishment. My old instructor's comment was, "I don't know how you did it, but if you complete primary, you'll wash out in basic." Really nice guy! In primary I flew 65 hours dual and solo, including cross country and aerobatics. As I recall, about half of those who started the primary flight school class at Cuero completed the course.

Basic Training

Of the seven students starting with my initial primary instructor, I was the only one to complete primary. What my instructor had said to me in Cuero, his undermining of my confidence and his prediction of failure had its effect on me. When starting basic training at Waco, I was very happy to be there but I was having difficulty because of my concern. I was slow to solo even though the instructors in basic were military pilots, and I felt much more comfortable with the relationship. My instructor didn't say much and was hard to read. One day he said, "You're going to have to solo pretty soon, and you seem to have a problem." I related my story. My recollection is vague but the advice was generally, "You're okay, you can handle it, forget about primary." Whatever he said, I felt reassured, soon soloed and had no further problem. In basic we were flying a single engine Vultee aircraft, a BT-13 A, known as the Vultee Vibrator. It had a sliding canopy and was way ahead of the PT-19, with 450 horsepower, compared with 175 hp for the PT-19, but I never liked the BT-13. It seemed like an awkward plane and was too noisy; it was like an overweight bumblebee. My flight log showed that I flew 90.8 hours, including dual and solo, day and night cross-country, aerobatics and instrument flying in the BT-13 A and made 175 landings.

Advanced Flying School

Advanced Flying School also was in Waco, at Blackland Army Air Field. I was very happy to stay in Waco because we had a group of congenial student officers who hung out together, and were having a good time. Through attending church I met a number of local people including several attractive young women whom I dated. The family of one of the girls had a home on the lake and gave parties there. Dinner dances were held at the officers club. At these functions the officers wore white dress uniforms and the ladies wore long dresses. Although these were formal occasions, the era was also one of "juke joints," roadside places that had a juke box. Musical selections for listening or dancing could be played for a quarter. A favorite at the time for listening was "Paper Doll."

We were learning to fly a twin-engine Beech aircraft, AT-10, with Lycoming engines, and 590 horsepower. I missed the aerobatics, which couldn't be performed in twin engine aircraft, but I was more inclined toward bombers than fighters. Essentially, I was too tall to feel comfortable in a small fighter cockpit, and being gregarious I liked flying with another pilot. It was fun. I had a wonderful time, enjoyed the flying and at the end of the course received my Silver Wings. I was a first lieutenant in the Army Air Corps! My parents were able to be present at the graduation and I asked my father to pin on my wings. He was then retiring from the Army after 36 years of service, at the age of 60.

Graduation

Typically, with any graduation one has mixed feelings. Graduation is both an ending and a beginning. At this time, in October 1943, there was a war raging in Europe and we were a group of eager young pilots who wanted to go out to win it. We had completed a difficult course of flight training and were now rated pilots. The future was unknown. We said good-bye to the young women of Waco and to our friends and fellow students. I never saw any of them again. A big mistake years later was going back to Waco to visit. Everyone I knew was gone. It was a very sad place, and I did not stay long.

But then I was beginning a great adventure. My assignment was Lakeland, Florida, to join a B-26 Martin Marauder group which was then in the final phase of operational training for combat. It would have been preferable to go to a B-26 transition school first, but there was a need for pilots in Europe and in the 344th Bombardment Group to which I was assigned. Omitting B-26 transition training made it possible for me to go overseas much sooner but made the adjustment to flying the B-26 Marauder more difficult. Most of what I learned was self-taught or learned on the job. There wasn't time for training and aircraft generally were not available for training either in Lakeland or in the U.K.

CHAPTER FIVE

TRAINING FOR WAR

Lakeland, Florida

The locations selected by the Army for training fields usually were in areas of the country where the flying weather was generally good. These locations included Texas and Florida. Following training in Texas, I drew Florida. After a short period of leave in San Antonio I left for Florida in the Buick. My assignment was Lakeland, near Orlando, with a B-26 Marauder group that was engaged in operational training prior to going into combat.

Transition training for the B-26 Martin Marauder was in Tampa, not far from Lakeland, where the B-26 had developed a reputation for being dangerous. The B-26 had a short wingspan; the resultant reduction of lift required higher speeds for takeoff and landing, and increased the danger - especially on takeoff if the aircraft lost an engine. There were a number of crashes.

In Lakeland the November weather was colder than I had anticipated. At night the low temperature made my room uncomfortable and there was no central heat in the building where I lived. This time I actually had quarters on the base, but I hardly remember them. My concentration was on learning about B-26 operations, and on having a good time before leaving for the European Theater of War. My disappointment in being unable to go through transition training to learn to fly the aircraft was countered by my excitement. We were undergoing operational training for combat!

The Oddball

As a first lieutenant just out of flight school I was in an unusual position. Because of my grade and lack of transition training, I was assigned as copilot with the crew of a captain, who was a flight commander. He had been a civilian pilot before going into the service, had a lot of flight time and had also driven racing cars. He was taciturn, with apparent nerves of steel, and an excellent pilot. I didn't feel comfortable with him, however, and we were never friends, but I felt that I could learn from him and that I would be safe flying with him.

Operational Training

My recall of operational training is limited. As a copilot I didn't have responsibility for the aircraft. The pilot rarely let me take the controls, which I resented, and sitting in the right seat as copilot was generally boring. One memorable aspect was flying low level - and we flew really low. Obviously this type of flying is dangerous, but it's also thrilling. When flying close to the ground you can feel the speed; speed and danger are exhilarating.

Before tactics for the B-26 Marauder had really been worked out for the European theater, it was thought that the aircraft would be most effective at low-level. That was considered true until a B-26 group was wiped out on the second low-level raid over Holland. By the time I started flying combat in 1944 our missions were flown at 10,000 to 12,000 feet. We didn't fly low-level missions, but we did train for them.

Vacating a Stadium

One low-level training flight was memorable. We had been dodging trees and electric transmission lines. Coming to a clear area we dropped low to the ground. At the end of the clear area there were stadium seats. A small group of men was sitting on the seats, eating lunch. Our Martin Marauder came roaring in, rising in elevation to get over the stadium seats. From the seats it must have been frightening to see this monster aircraft unexpectedly approaching at eye level. After the initial shock the men scrambled to get down on the ground. Probably at the very least the incident ruined their lunch.

Joining the Caterpillar Club

The most dramatic event occurred during a medium-level training flight. We had to jump, BAIL OUT! We had been flying at 10,000 feet near Sarasota but had descended to about 4,000 feet with neither engine then operating when the Captain gave the order to bail out. The radio operator asked, "Who goes first?" My response was, "You do!" I gave him a gentle shove out the bomb bay. He always remembered that and we had a lot of laughs. As I remembered, that was the order of precedence. I had often wondered what it would feel like to parachute from a plane. During flight training I had asked the question about what to do and was told, "You'll find out when you have to do it." That was poor advice and the instruction was later changed.

I was not afraid of the jump at the time but was concerned about doing it right. The copilot is the last one out before the captain; he was still at the controls when I left the aircraft. I stepped out through the bomb bay on the way to membership in the Caterpillar Club. This club required a lifesaving parachute jump as qualification for membership. I was awarded a Caterpillar Club pin. As I bailed out, my concern was to avoid being hit by the tail section and to clear the plane before pulling the ripcord to open the chute. Both tasks were accomplished, thanks be to God.

After jumping from the plane, hanging out in the atmosphere was an odd feeling with no sensation of speed or of falling. When I pulled the ripcord of my parachute I felt a strong jerk as the chute opened. As the plane was at 4,000 feet when I jumped, it seemed that a long time was required to reach the ground after the chute opened. It was like sitting in a swing. I didn't see any other chutes but did observe the plane as it went down; it looked as though it were being piloted and I thought that the captain had decided to try an emergency landing. The plane landed on a field and then flipped forward into a total ball of flame. (He had bailed out.)

By that time I was nearing the ground which was coming up quite fast. Drifting sideways, I endeavored, in order to face forward for landing, to turn the chute by pulling on the supports, or risers. I believe that I spilled the air from the chute about 50 feet in the air, and I landed with a thud. Upon hitting the ground I could neither breathe nor move under my own power, but was being dragged by the chute. After a minute or two I could breathe again — the wind had just been knocked out of me — but I still couldn't move and thought that my back was broken. Gradually I was able to get to my feet and remove the chute. Slowly I started walking toward the flames I could see from the burning aircraft.

The crash had been reported at the base with the indication that there were no survivors. A meeting was being held at the base at that time for all personnel, a meeting we were supposed to attend, but we were otherwise engaged. The announcement of the crash and the grossly exaggerated report of our demise were made at the meeting. The word got back to Betty, the young woman from Lakeland whom I was dating at the time.

Fire engines and ambulances arrived at the location of the plane about the same time I did. I sat down and then couldn't get up again, so I was taken by ambulance with sirens blaring to the base hospital. Very exciting! My face was beaten up and bloody from my being dragged by the chute after landing, so I looked as if I were returning from combat rather than preparing for it. A crowd of people was standing by the entrance to the hospital. They looked concerned and sympathetic and I managed to look appropriately pitiful.

The hospital admitted me on December 23, 1943. My last Christmas before going overseas was spent in the hospital! The X-rays showed no apparent broken bones. The diagnosis was a "bad lumbar sprain." The attending physician advised that I needed to rest and to stay in bed or in a wheelchair. He said that I would be reassigned as the group was leaving shortly for the POE (port of embarkation). I did not want to be left behind! I wanted to go overseas with the group.

It seemed appropriate to call my mother in San Antonio so I could tell her what had happened before she heard it from someone else. When she answered the telephone, I said, "Do you remember when I told you that I always wanted to bail out of a plane?" She didn't seem too shook up, inasmuch as I was okay. Naturally my physician walked by just as I was leaving the phone booth. He growled, "I thought I told you to stay in a wheelchair!" "It wouldn't fit in the phone booth," I responded.

Betty first heard about the plane crash and was very upset, then later that we had survived and I was in the hospital. She came by to visit and to see if there was anything she could do. "I'd like a dry martini," I said, "but I don't know how you could bring one into the hospital." "I'll think of something," she said. On return that evening she brought a small crystal bud vase with a single rose. Each evening she brought another single rose in the bud vase. The hospital staff thought it was a touching display of affection. Each evening I removed the rose from the vase and enjoyed the contents — a dry, properly chilled martini. Fortunately the roses didn't wilt before their arrival at the hospital.

Release From the Hospital

Although my back was bothering me, I convinced the doc that I was ready to return to duty. After four or five days I was released from the hospital and returned to the group. Even though my back still bothers me now, at the time it was better to be hurting than to go overseas on my own as a replacement pilot. I had friends in the squadron and in the small-world department, the group commander, Colonel Reginald F. C. Vance, was from San Antonio. He flew back to San Antonio for a short last visit before going overseas and I was invited to go with him, for which I was very grateful.

Colonel Vance was famous as a pilot flying U.S. dive bombers in the Philippines until none remained and then fighting at Bataan and Corregidor with General Douglas MacArthur's staff. General MacArthur ordered 200 pounds of gold removed from the last departing submarine to enable Colonel Vance to leave. He was considered worth his weight in gold.

Congratulations . . .

It is indeed a pleasure to welcome you as a member of the Caterpillar Club.

As is customary, we are having the official insignia of the Club made and engraved especially for you. Unfortunately, however, due to supply restrictions, this may not be received for several months, but will be sent to you at the first opportunity.

In the meantime we have pleasure in sending your membership certificate, which you will find attached. with our best wishes, in recognition of the emergency parachute jump which you made.

CATERPILLAR CLUB

CHAPTER SIX

EN ROUTE TO WAR

Savannah

Long before the popular novel and movie, "Midnight in the Garden of Good and Evil," came on the scene, my squadron was in Savannah, Georgia, en route to a base in Britain and combat in the European Theater of War. Savannah was the staging area or aerial port of embarkation, the last stop for us before leaving the States. We were in Savannah for a week or two for briefings and preparation for departure. The equipment needed for the flight across the Atlantic and for the European Theater where we were headed was issued to us and loaded aboard our aircraft, a B-26 Marauder. Life rafts were important pieces of equipment when flying across the Atlantic, and "Mae Wests" were also crucial to survival if we had to ditch, or crash land, on the water. "Mae West" was the name given to the individual life vest because of its supposed resemblance to the torso of the actress when the vest was inflated. A flight suit and leather jacket, a flak vest and steel helmet and a backpack parachute were part of the wardrobe of the well-dressed combat pilot. Flak vests were heavy and awkward to wear but comforting and protective. The steel helmets were uncomfortable but they were lifesaving equipment. Abandoned were the white scarves and leather headgear of flight school. One luxurious piece of equipment was a marvelously soft bedroll. But I never got to use it. Not once! More about that later.

During this last respite, before heading south, to Puerto Rico and to South America, and then on to Africa and Western Europe, we had a lot of spare time and freedom to go out on the town. We were staying in a hotel, which was an unaccustomed luxury. There were other aircrews to hang out with, and the local bars received heavy patronage. Bowling with friends, including a fellow pilot who looked something like the character in the comic strip *Joe Palooka*, occupied part of the time. "Joe" was an expert bowler and an aficionado of the sport. One evening a group of us were at a bar with "Joe" and he was getting a bit out of order, having overindulged in the suds. We couldn't get him to leave and he was big enough to prevent any of us from forcing him out. I came up with the brilliant suggestion that we go bowling, because he liked the sport so much. The idea of bowling appealed to him so off we went to a bowling alley. Although he had a bit of trouble standing, he got a better bowling score than I did. At that moment I vowed never to bowl again and I haven't.

Johnny

A young pilot and friend, Johnny Dye, who was twenty or twenty-one, had gotten married just before we left for Savannah. Understandably, he was not happy about leaving his bride to go overseas, but he seemed more depressed than unhappy. One evening Johnny confided to me that he knew he was not coming back from the war. I tried to convince him that none of us had any way of knowing for sure whether we would survive the war but that it was far better to believe that we would. "I know I'm coming back," I said. As far as I could determine, what I said to him then didn't have any effect, but after we arrived in Britain, Johnny always seemed cheerful. I thought he was okay. Unfortunately, he knew a truth that was later evidenced to me in a strange twist of fate.

Farewell to my Buick

While in Savannah I had to sell my beloved Buick. It was a blue two-passenger coupe with a lot of space behind the seat and in the large trunk. The Buick had been with me from age nineteen in San Antonio, from my first station in Texas, at Camp Bowie, on to Fort Benning, Georgia, to Fort Jackson, South Carolina, Fort Hood, Texas, through flight training in Cuero and Waco, and on to Lakeland, Florida. On departing a station I could stash all my belongings in one footlocker, throw the footlocker in the car trunk and be ready to roll. There was room for a friend's baggage as well if the friend was going my way. Jack Dillon was in my flight class in Waco and I dropped him off at his home on the Gulf Coast en route to Florida. Jack was always laughing and jovial. I had met his wife and liked both of them. After leaving Jack I drove on alone to Lakeland. Later I learned in a letter from Jack's wife that he had been killed in a vehicular accident.

Savannah, Georgia was the end of the road for my Buick. Because I couldn't take the car with me, it had to go, or I should say stay. But selling the car was like parting with a good and faithful friend. That automobile was a joy to drive and totally reliable.

The Buick was sold for less than it was worth. There wasn't time to negotiate and I did not have a good bargaining position, as everyone in the Savannah area knew we were leaving the country. I had earned the money and paid cash to buy my first car, which made me proud of it. The Buick was sacrificed for the war effort, after providing effective transportation, a lot of fun, and a number of memories.

On to Puerto Rico and South America

Because of the limited range of the B-26 Marauder, additional fuel tanks were installed for the flight to England. It was still necessary to fly a circuitous route to get there. From Savannah we flew to Puerto Rico, landing at Borinquen Field and spending the night. We had frozen daiquiris on the terrace of the officers' mess, the last pleasant evening until Marrakech. The next day we flew on to Georgetown, British Guiana, then to Belem and Natal, Brazil. Leaving British Guiana, we were flying low along the coast headed east toward Belem when we encountered tropical monsoon rain. The rain was the densest, heaviest downpour we had ever seen or flown in. The rain made it virtually impossible to see anything outside the cockpit, including landmarks. All that was visible were the angry waves, impenetrable tropical forest and torrential rain. Because the aircraft was low on fuel we were beginning to be very concerned. We had to find our destination quickly. Finally I spotted the wide mouth of a river, The Amazon, intersecting the coastline. Following the river south led us to the airfield. There was no margin for error and there were moments when we thought this flight would be the end of the story. Several legs of the flight seemed to have built-in major hazards but then so did the destination — the European Theater of War.

An Elusive Island

Having completed the flight from British Guiana to Belem and then to Natal, our next stop en route to Africa was Ascension Island, a small island located in the middle of the Atlantic. As we flew across the Atlantic there were no landmarks and our navigational equipment was limited to a radio direction finder, an instrument on the panel like a compass with an arrow that would point to the radio station when in range; the range was relatively short. Theoretically the plane would be headed for the station when it's nose was in line with the arrow, which was lined up with the zero point of the instrument. A crosswind you were unaware of, however, could result in your flying past the station. It was appropriate to correct the course if you knew the direction of the wind and the wind speed. Another factor limiting the value of the instrument was that sometimes it wasn't possible to pick up the radio signal. Some crews had been advised not to rely on the radio direction finder because German submarines were putting out false signals.

The wind was not as stated in the weather briefing in Natal. We were off course but didn't know it; the wind was blowing us north of our course. Before taking off, it is usually necessary to make a flight plan. A typical flight plan includes the estimated time over each checkpoint and the estimated time of arrival, or ETA, at the destination. There were no check points on this flight, just the Atlantic ocean. We had almost reached our ETA; the island was not in sight and we were low on fuel. We had not been able to pick up the radio signal. There was no place other than Ascension Island to land besides the water. Finally we got a weak radio signal. The needle of the direction finder was almost 90 degrees off to the right.

During our training we were told to "believe the instruments." In this case there was only one instrument to believe, the direction finder. We believed! Soon we saw Ascension Island. After flying low over the field to chase the birds off the runway, we landed. We were very glad to land on the runway; the alternative was not appealing.

Two pilots from our squadron while with another organization flying B-26s via the South Atlantic route to North Africa in 1943 failed to reach their destination. On the flight from Natal to Ascension, the B-26 flown by Captain Cletus Wray developed engine trouble and lost the right engine about 300 miles out. The bomb-bay tanks were dropped to lighten the load, but then the bomb-bay doors would not close. Unable to hold altitude with one engine, Wray was forced to ditch in the Atlantic. All members of the crew survived the crash landing. Lieutenant Harvey Johnson flew around the crash site to report the location before continuing on to Ascension. But the Atlantic is a large ocean. It was only after four and a half days floating in a rubber life raft, that the crew was rescued by the *USS Marblehead*. The story of life on the raft was told by John Guiher, the navigator-bombardier, in 344th Bomb Group (M), History and Remembrances, World War II, edited by Lambert D. Austin. Guiher tells a touching story of their difficulties after the crash and while on the raft.

The plane piloted by Lieutenant Harvey Johnson went on to Ascension. Departing from Ascension, Johnson's plane crashed in the Atlantic about 40 miles out after an engine failure. Johnson was the only survivor; all the other crew members perished. He floated in a Mae West until rescued. Both pilots, Wray and Johnson, were returned to the United States and reassigned to the 344th Bomb Group.

Stranger than fiction, Guiher was with Johnson, then a Captain, when his plane was shot down, April 20, 1944. The copilot was flying in my stead. I had been scheduled to fly with Johnson but because of a conflicting duty, which is explained later, I did not fly with him.

Arrival in Africa

The next stop in our Atlantic crossing was in Africa, Roberts Field, Liberia. The flight from Ascension was uneventful, a welcome change. After landing and upon leaving the aircraft I was thirsty but didn't know where to get a drink of potable water. A small boy was standing nearby watching us. Believing it unlikely that he would speak English, I pointed to my mouth and then made a motion as though drinking from a cup. He responded in perfect English, "If you want a drink of water, there's a Lister bag (canvas water bag) hanging on the tree over there."

The Desert Crossing

Our next scheduled flight was from Liberia to Marrakech, French Morocco, via Dakar, a long and difficult flight across the Sahara. As usual the wind forecast was not accurate. The headwind was stronger than anticipated. For a reason I don't recall, Johnny Guiher, the squadron commander's navigator was flying with us on this leg. Johnny was a very likable guy, and a bit of a character. The aircraft was heavily loaded and having trouble maintaining altitude. The captain made the observation that if we did not want to land in the desert, all baggage and equipment not absolutely necessary would have to be sacrificed, thrown out through the bomb bay. He directed Johnny and the rest of the crew to dump everything that wasn't part of the plane. It was very painful to see all those items that we had carefully loaded, including our limited personal belongings, being thrown out. "What about the bedrolls?" Johnny asked. "Out," the captain ordered. "We can get replacements in Britain." (He was so wrong! None were available in Britain and I was miserable for the duration of combat, especially in France.) Finally, Johnny came forward to the cockpit to announce that everything was gone, including the baggage. "All of it?" the captain asked. Johnny said, "You mean that you want me to throw mine out too?" "YES!" the captain thundered. After flying over miles and miles of desert sand we arrived in Dakar. Later it was on to Marrakech.

A Visit to the Casbah

We spent three weeks in Marrakech waiting for favorable winds for the final leg of the flight to Britain. It was essential that we fly far enough off the coast of Portugal to avoid being shot down by the antiaircraft guns located there, and sufficiently far off the French coast to avoid German fighters operating from France. These restrictions made the flight longer than it otherwise would have been.

In Marrakech we were living in tents but spent time at the Hotel Maumonia, a hotel that normally catered to wealthy Europeans. It was a beautiful place and we liked spending time there but ultimately it became boring. In my February 5, 1944, letter to my parents I wrote, "It's hot in daytime and cold as the devil at night...I've been using four blankets and my winter flying suit at night to cover up with...I've been going to town at night and eating at the hotel. The food is pretty good. It costs about 70 francs or $1.40. They serve wine with every meal — all you want. It isn't very good wine, though. War is hell. You certainly appreciate things now that you formerly took for granted, such as hot showers, radios, heat, food, automobiles, chairs and tables, beds and numerous other things — in fact most anything. Our home seems like a palace from where I sit. I'm getting tired of living out of a barracks bag. Haven't had any laundry or cleaning for a month and everything I own is filthy."

One night two friends and I hired a driver to take us to the Casbah, the walled city. When we arrived in the city, the driver announced that he was charging double the fare that he had agreed to for the trip. If we declined to pay the increased fare as he asked, he threatened to leave us in the Casbah. We agreed to pay him at that time one half the fare he demanded and to pay the other half when we were back where we started, at the Maumonia. He said, "Okay." We thought that two could play at this game. When we were back at the starting point, we told the driver to take a hike. We had paid the fare as originally agreed. Fortunately we were neither knifed nor shot.

As for the Casbah, it was intriguing but not a place where it was comfortable to be. From my letter of February 6, 1944: "The only excitement I've had is going into the native village. It is a maze of walls, narrow streets, alleys and houses built adjoining each other for blocks. It's really a puzzle finding your way in and out. We had a native guide. It was pretty scary being in there at night with hooded men lurking in every corner." Everything was different — street vendors, narrow passageways, dark corners, and strange people in the shadows.

The Red Cross

In a letter from Marrakech, I wrote, "I appreciate the Red Cross since I left the States. They've given us cigarettes, candy, cards, stationery and other things. They have a beautiful building for a Red Cross Service Center. It's for enlisted men, but we can go in and take a hot shower. The first since leaving the States. I think that it is a wonderful organization. They're doing a fine job."

The Flight to the U.K.

The time arrived when the winds were forecast to be favorable for the last leg of our long journey, from North Africa to the U.K. As usual, the wind forecast was inaccurate. We flew and flew and continued to fly for hours. Darkness began to descend and a storm was brewing. Our fuel supply was low. We could see nothing but heavy waves in the encroaching darkness. Our ETA was long past and no shoreline was in sight. We began calling MAYDAY, MAYDAY, the international distress call.

Suddenly I had a glimpse of the cliffs along the coast of England near Lands End. An airfield not far from the coast had heard our distress call, was cognizant of our plight and made the decision to defy the blackout and turn the runway lights on briefly. Never did it feel so great to be back on the ground. Never have I been so cold as I was that night! The weather was windy, damp and cold, the penetrating, bone-chilling type of cold. How I wished that I had my bedroll, which was somewhere on the Sahara keeping the desert rats warm. It was a miserable night, except for the fact that we were on the ground and we were almost at our destination. The next morning we flew on to Stansted, the base where the 344th Bomb Group was assigned, near Bishops Stortford, about 30 miles north of London.

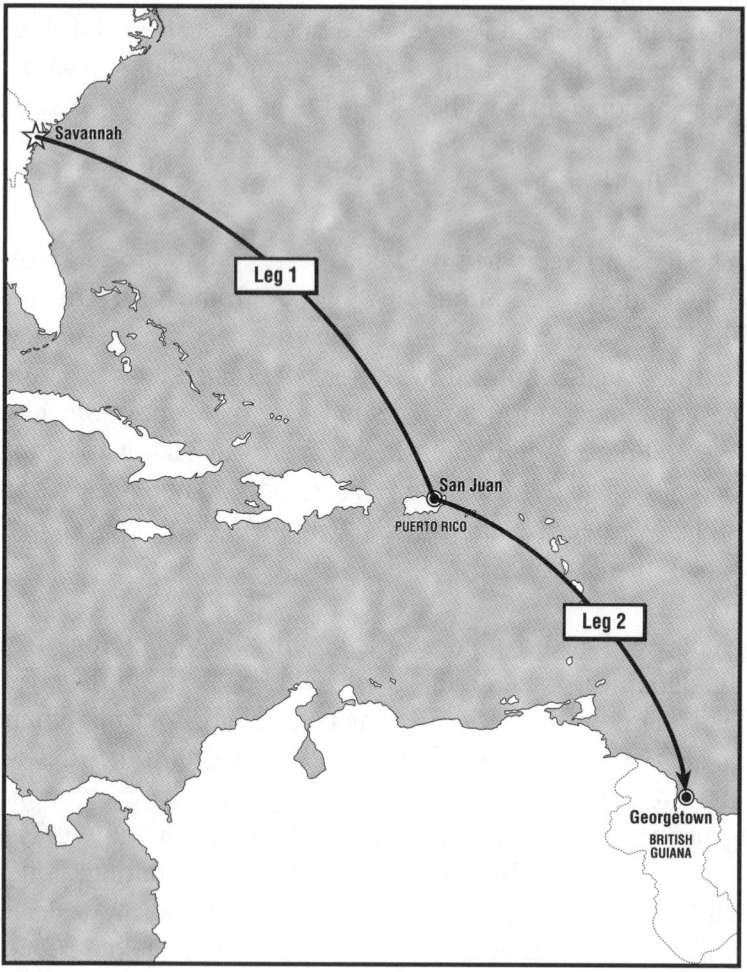
Savannah
Leg 1
San Juan
PUERTO RICO
Leg 2
Georgetown
BRITISH
GUIANA

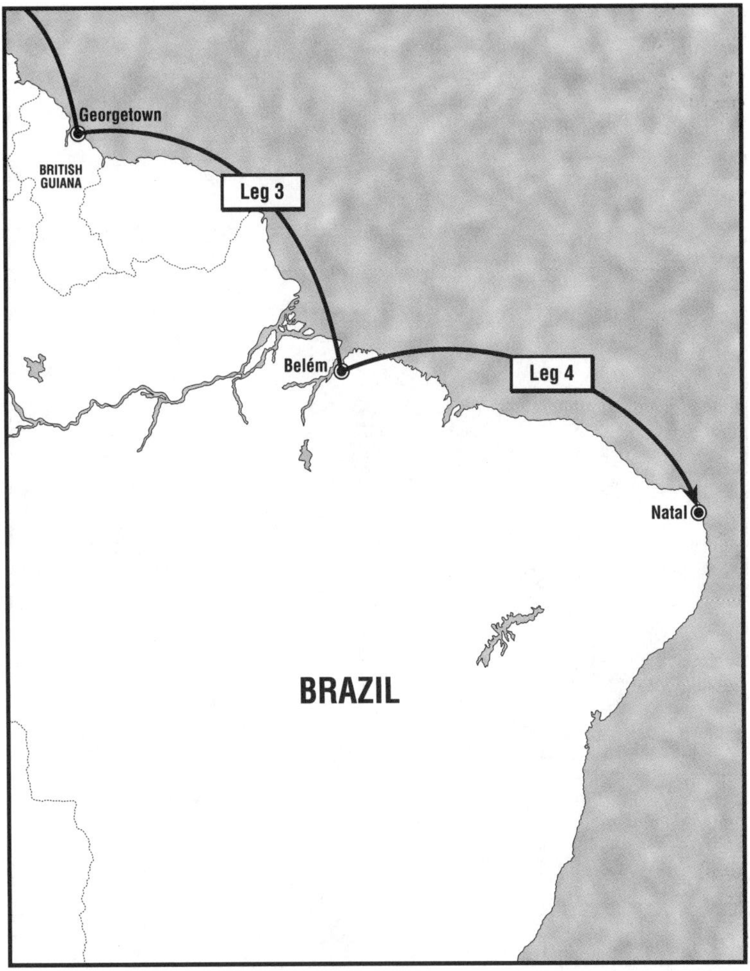
Georgetown
BRITISH GUIANA
Leg 3
Belém
Leg 4
Natal
BRAZIL

78

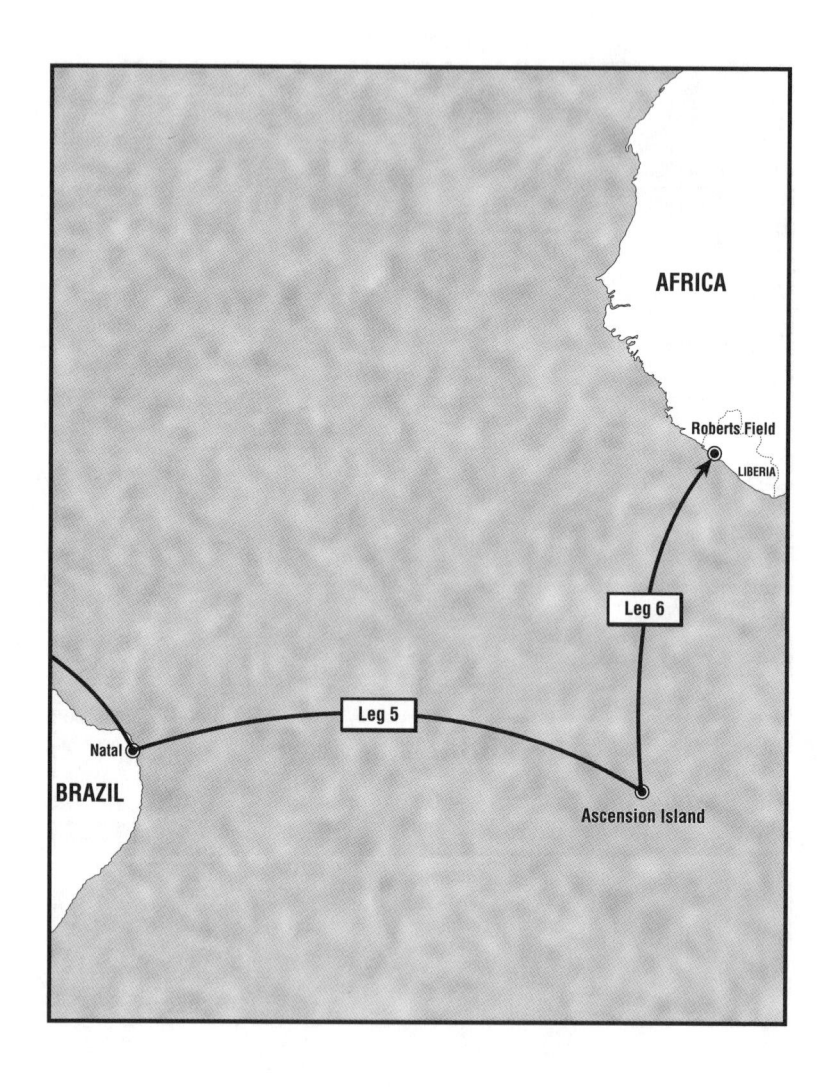

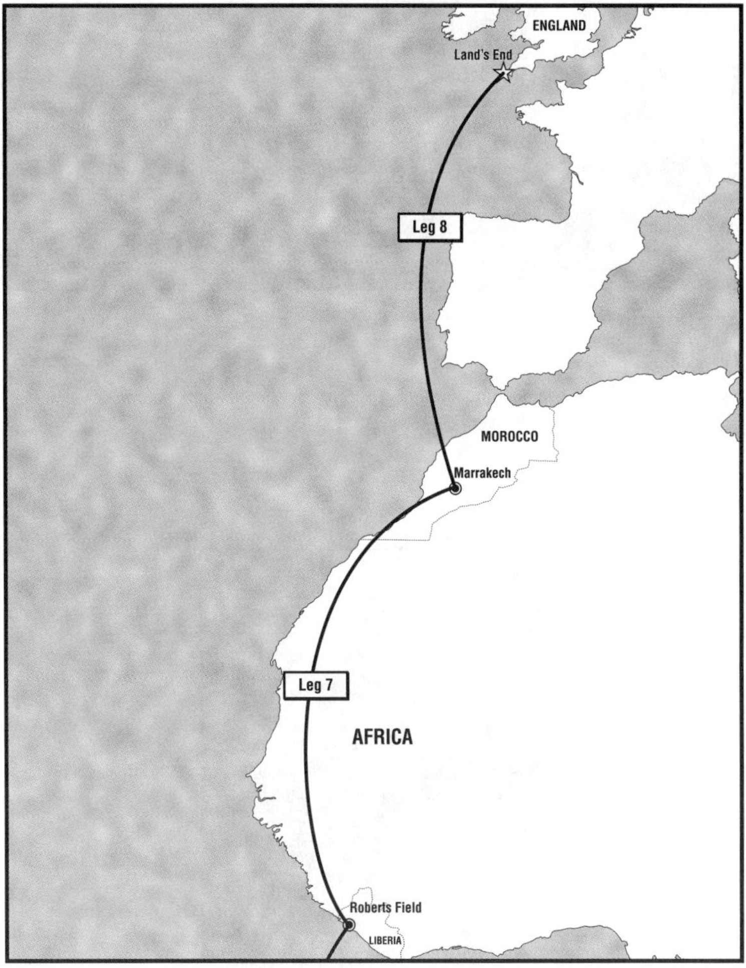
ENGLAND
Land's End
Leg 8
MOROCCO
Marrakech
Leg 7
AFRICA
Roberts Field
LIBERIA

Mamounia Hotel

My first Buick

CHAPTER SEVEN

BASED IN BRITAIN

Base Housing

Nissen or Quonset huts had been constructed on the base at Stansted to house the group personnel. The huts were made of corrugated-steel sections in the shape of a half moon fastened to concrete slabs. The ends of the huts were enclosed with a door at one end and windows. Bunks were lined up on both sides of the hut with an aisle in the center. Over the head of each bunk a shelf was provided for personal belongings. In my case personal belongings were limited, with most of them stored somewhere on the Sahara. Along the side of each hut, trenches two or three feet deep had been dug to provide air-raid shelter. Bathrooms and showers were nearby.

On the base there was a mess hall (dining hall) where our meals were served and an officers' club. Our life on the base was quite civilized. It seemed odd to fly combat missions, drop bombs and get shot at and then return to the base and don dress uniform for dinner at the officers' mess. Existence became schizophrenic. For a while we were allowed to wear flight suits to dinner but everyone started getting sloppy and morale took a dive, so we were ordered back to uniforms.

Bicycles were issued to flight crews primarily for transportation to the flight line, but we could use them to go to other destinations. On many evenings we rode our bicycles into Bishops Stortford to visit one of the pubs. Pleasant evenings playing darts, drinking beer and conversing helped release tension. The trip back to base could be awkward in the blackout, especially if the road turned and your bicycle didn't. Don Iddins, a friend and fellow pilot in the 496th, and I failed to see a turn in the road and rode into a haystack. No harm was done to either of us or to the bicycles. We thought the incident was tremendously funny.

On March 2, 1944, I wrote, "This is Texas Independence

Day, isn't it? It seems that independence and freedom are something you must fight to maintain. Others gave up their lives so that I was able to enjoy life in the United States. So as I see it, it's up to me to risk mine to help keep what they fought for."

The Buzz Stops Here!

The location of real estate is of prime importance. One of the flaws in our base location was that Stansted was on the flight path of the German flying bombs. The pulse-jet-powered secret weapons, V-1s, part aircraft, part bomb, were called "buzz bombs." They were launched from Belgium and France. Their target was London, but some of them flew over London and across our base at a low altitude. The buzz bombs made a distinctive sound that was easy to recognize, something like a certain type of helicopter. As long as the sound of the buzz bomb was audible you were relatively safe. When the engine stopped, the sound also stopped and the bomb came down. Upon impact the bomb could cause a lot of damage to the surrounding area. When a bomb hit nearby, the blast would knock everything off the shelves above the bunks. If you were in your bunk everything would drop on your head; profanity ensued.

The first time we had an air-raid warning I went out to lie down in one of the trenches. The trench was cold, damp and decidedly uncomfortable. My bunk was comfortable. Therefore I decided that if in the future I were in my bunk, I would stay there. If a bomb hit I would at least be comfortable and not cold, damp and muddy.

In London I made a similar decision. The shelters in the tube stations were crowded, noisy and unpleasant. My hotel room was much more pleasant, so I stayed there or wherever I happened to be when the warning sounded.

Assignment

My assignment in Britain was as a pilot with the 496th Squadron, 344th Bombardment Group, 9th Bombardment division, 99th Wing, 9th Air Force. The Bomb Group comprised four Squadrons, the 494th, 495th, 496th and 497th. The squadrons comprised flights of six aircraft each. The squadron commander was a lieutenant colonel as was the squadron operations officer. Both were rated pilots (the term used for officers who completed flight qualification and were then "rated"). Flight commanders were captains. Most of the pilots were first or second lieutenants.

The squadron executive officer was a major, non-rated, and the adjutant was a captain, also nonrated. Other positions in maintenance and engineering also did not require a flight rating. The officers responsible for these two functions were captains. The table of organization, or TO, prescribed the grade authorized for various positions. It seemed to the flying officers that the nonrated officers had a better shot at promotion than we did. If they were assigned the position, they could go from second lieutenant to captain in six months, whereas many of the pilots went overseas as second or first lieutenants, completed a combat tour and returned to the States in the same grade.

The squadron commander, Lieutenant Colonel Jewell C. Maxwell, from Tennessee, was tough, blunt and assertive and a superb pilot. When he led the group, it was easy to fly his wing because he held the aircraft and airspeed steady and never wavered. He became a major general before retiring from the Air Force. His last assignment was heading the Air Force supersonic-jet transport project.

The operations officer, Cletus Wray, was a major when we arrived in England, and was soon promoted to lieutenant colonel. Also from Tennessee, he was a big guy, a football type, who ran squadron operations well. He was easier to talk to than Maxwell, but not usually available. In the beginning he and I didn't have much contact.

One night Wray and his bombardier, Henry Florsheim, came into the hut just after I had gone to sleep. They had been visiting the local pub and were slightly looped. Henry said after waking me up, "I'm going to punch you in the eye." I told him to get lost, but he persisted and finally I said, "Get out of here!" To make him get out, as he suggested, I personally escorted him out the door. As I stepped into the dark, not able to see very well, Wray gave me a push backward and I tripped over a bicycle. Angrily I got up and took a swing at him. Fortunately someone got between us, probably saving me from being killed, and I went back to bed.

By then I was awake and thought, "My God, what have I done? Assaulting a senior officer is a courts-martial offense. This may be the end of my Air Force career."

The next day as I pondered my fate and wondered what I should do, I was summoned to Wray's office. Expecting the worst, I was surprised to hear him apologize for what had occurred. He told me, "Henry and I had a little too much to drink last night." I readily accepted his apology and offered mine.

As we conversed, he asked, "Where did you screw up?" "What do you mean?" I responded. He said, "Well, you're a first lieutenant and still a copilot." I suggested that if he reviewed my record, he would note that I had gone through pilot training as a first lieutenant, as a student officer, and was assigned directly to the B-26 Marauder Group from flight school, without having had the opportunity to go through transition. On arrival at Lakeland I was assigned as copilot to a captain.

Wray changed his attitude toward me, saying that he would get me checked out as a first pilot, and give me a crew. He followed through. I was checked out and had six hours in the left seat when I flew my first mission as first pilot. Subsequently, when I had flown a number of missions, he submitted a recommendation for my promotion to captain and flight commander, after a flight commander was shot down. It disturbed me that the opening came about as it did, but that is the way it was. I felt better when my predecessor, Captain John Hegg, returned to visit the group some months later after escaping and making his way back to England. When he saw me he said, with his usual sarcastic humor, "I see they've raised the TO for copilots." He was sent back to the States as were all those who were shot down and escaped.

A Prescribed Combat Tour

The prescribed tour in Europe for B-26 Marauder crews when we arrived in the U.K. was 50 combat missions; later this limit was removed, which created morale and other problems. A tour was then set at 65 missions. Each pilot and crew had a specific aircraft assigned to them, which they flew unless their assigned aircraft was damaged, grounded for engineering reasons, or shot down while another crew was flying it. This system worked well as the flight crews became familiar with their particular aircraft and took pride in its performance. Many of the pilots gave a name to their plane and often commissioned an appropriate painting for the fuselage of the plane. The planes I flew were "Six Hits and a Miss," for the flight crew of six and the aircraft, and "Lily Marlene," named after a popular song.

Usually a bomb replica was painted on the side of the fuselage to represent each combat mission the aircraft had flown. Each plane also had an official letter and number designation on the tail. One plane was designated "K-9 P" — "K-9," to designate the squadron, and "P," to designate the plane. This evolved into "canine pee," and the plane was referred to derogatorily by other crews as "dog piss."

Relaxing in front of a nissen hut

TEXAS STARS IN BRITISH SKIES

Watching the skies for returning planes are these three San Antonio pilots of Marauder medium bombers at a base somewhere in England.

Left to right: First Lieut. Frank W. Bauers Jr., Capt V. A. Smith and Capt. Howard L. Burris (in cockpit.)

From San Antonio newspaper

Six Hits and a Miss

CHAPTER EIGHT

LIFE IN THE U.K.

The British Pub, the Club and the Public

On days that our crew wasn't scheduled to fly, we had freedom of the base. If we didn't have to fly the following day, we would ride our bicycles into Bishops Stortford in the blackout and spend some time at the local pub, drinking warm beer. In the beginning warm beer or ale seemed awful, but we got used to it. The pubs were atmospheric and the people were friendly, although we suspected that they would just as soon have us return to the United States. The pub was like a club, where the local people got together. Most of them knew one other and had a convivial time and pleasant evening.

We also had an officers club on the base. From a letter of March 18, 1944, "Dear Dad, I just came back to the barracks from the club. Practically broke my neck trying to ride a bike back in this blackout. I have never seen anything blacker than one of these nights in England, and there is not a light to behold. It isn't very far from here, but I couldn't see a thing. Where the road turned, I didn't, then finally wound up in a concrete mixer, and a great deal of concrete. It was a hard fight, but I made it!

"Our club is a large room built on to the mess hall. It's pretty nice for over here. Has a large fireplace on either end, numerous chairs and couches (second hand) and a bar. They are selling sandwiches and cakes now too, and they have a few books. It is very much appreciated. I've learned to appreciate the simple things in life. I'd rather stay on the base, sit by the fire and read or write letters, than go to town.

"Up to now I haven't met many of the British people but I've seen what they have done and have a great admiration for them. They have had a long, bitter struggle and have had to make sacrifices and endure things that the Americans have not dreamed of. Everything, from the bread they eat to the clothes on their backs, is rationed. You see almost no cars on the road; they've all been put up for the duration. They have lived in a total blackout for years. They do without everything and don't gripe about it.

"I would like to fly more missions than I have been. I want to do everything I can to help get this over and destroy Hitler and his regime. There is a satisfaction in coming back from a mission and knowing you have accomplished something. I suppose a civilian would be surprised at seeing the attitude of this bunch. Everyone is eager to go on a mission, is more bored than excited, and has a complete disregard for the possible danger involved. You have too much to do while you're up in the air without doing much thinking. Besides I evidently don't have enough sense to get scared. Upon returning from a mission, the main thought in mind is food, then "the sack" (bunk). Along with it is the satisfaction that you've done a day's work."

48 Hours in London

Periodically we were given a 48-hour pass to London. It was a great release to get away from the base and into a different scene. From my letter of April 19, 1944, to my mother, "Had two days off and went to London. We (pilot, bombardier and I) left Sunday afternoon and came back last night... . It was a very quiet time, didn't do anything but see three shows, eat a few good meals, have a few, very few drinks, and sleep in a good bed. Although that wasn't very exciting, it was restful. We stayed at the Strand Palace hotel — not too expensive — cost us two pounds, ten shillings, for three of us for two nights. That is equivalent to ten dollars. Been eating at the officers' mess in London. There are two of them, one in the Grosvenor Hotel, one in the Junior Officers Club. You can get a meal for a half-crown (50 cents) which beats anything that you can buy in London in a restaurant. They just don't have any food… ."

London was about 30 miles from the base and the trains provided fast and generally excellent transportation. Usually the trains were very crowded and the seats in the compartments were filled. It was necessary to stand in the passageway, which was not unpleasant… . One day there was a beautiful young girl standing nearby who was traveling to London with her mother. We started a conversation that developed into a friendship with both mother and daughter. They lived near our base. Sylvia was a model and magazine cover girl. She was just 17, and I had attained the age of 23, so we didn't date, but I enjoyed her company when I visited them. Sylvia's mother was 37 and quite attractive and more interesting.

We didn't have the time or the opportunity to meet young women. I suspect that the parents did their best to prevent our meeting their daughters. Many of the young women were in military service. My friend Don Iddins did meet a lovely young woman, Molly, and after the war he returned to England and married her.

Usually I would go to London with a pilot friend from another squadron, Herb Engelbrecht, if he had a pass at the same time that I did, or with Harry Hague. As American officers we were given access to most of the clubs in London. For accommodations we would stay at one of the major hotels, especially the Dorchester, or a rental flat on Jermyn street which was available for short term rentals. There was little incentive for us to save money because of the nature of our employment, so we would live it up for 48 hours and then return to the war. Actually we never got away from the war because London was in blackout, and air raids were frequent. Once I went to a shelter in London, which was a tube (subway) station, but it was too crowded and uncomfortable. I formed the same conclusion about bomb shelters as I did about the ditch next to our hut. I elected to remain comfortable where I was at the time. There were a few shattered windows in the Jermyn Street apartment one night and the lights went out when bombs landed nearby.

One afternoon I decided to walk to Covent Garden. En route there I stopped to look at a shop window. Shortly after I stopped walking, while I was standing in front of the window, a bomb struck at Covent Garden, at the spot where I would have been had I kept walking. It seemed that I was being saved to further the war effort or for some other purpose.

London was an exciting place to visit. The British and American forces that were on duty or visiting in London generated a lot of action. Although the danger of bombings from manned aircraft had subsided, the buzz bombs and rockets were a present danger. Air raid sirens went off almost every night. Endeavoring to maneuver in a city in total blackout, one could encounter a problem. One night, which was so black I couldn't see anything, I accidentally bumped into a woman. She exclaimed, "I say, why don't you look where you're going!" I thought that her comment was exceedingly funny. There was a lot of destruction in London. Through it all the British remained stoic and resolute.

It was strange to see the lights upon returning to London after the war, but I was delighted that the damaged buildings had been rebuilt, those still standing had been cleaned and the city was shining.

R & R

After a number of missions I had the opportunity in August 1944 for a week of R & R at an English estate, which was beautiful, luxurious and well staffed. It was great having a bed, with sheets, breakfast in bed, and tea in the afternoon. The atmosphere was uplifting and the food was excellent. Being there was very restful and I enjoyed pretending that I lived there.

Several trips to Cambridge were possible. The weather was beautiful when I visited, and it was very peaceful sitting on the bank of the river. Since that time I have often been to Cambridge in my imagination, as a place of refuge.

A trip by train to Scotland to visit Aberdeen and Edinburgh was very enjoyable. When I arrived in Aberdeen, fog and mist rising two or three feet above the ground enveloped the city, making it appear ethereal. Other than being there and walking around I didn't do much but I appreciated the chance to see these two cities.

R&R location

Main Street, Bishops Stortford

First ship rolling

First ship in the air

CHAPTER NINE

COMBAT FLYING

The Martin B-26 Marauder

The Army had determined the need for a medium bomber with certain qualifications, and in January 1939, issued specifications to manufacturers for a twin-engine, five-place, medium bomber. It was to have the capacity to carry a 4,000-pound bomb load, with a range of 3,000 miles and speed of 250 to 350 miles per hour. The Glen L. Martin Co. appointed a young aeronautical engineer and designer, Peyton L. Magruder, as the project engineer. The Martin Co. won the competition in July 1939. The first B-26 came off the assembly line and had its maiden flight on November 25, 1940, a record time for development of an aircraft. The first four Martin B-26s were delivered to the Army Air Force at Langley Field, Virginia, on February 22, 1941. Because the engineering specifications had been changed and additional weight had been added, the speed and range of the aircraft were reduced from that originally specified.

As originally designed the B-26 had a 65-foot wingspan and a very high wing loading. When the planes were sent to AAF training fields, the combination of inexperienced pilots and relatively green aircraft mechanics led to a high accident rate. To provide greater lift and thus increase the aircraft's safety, the wingspan was increased from 65 to 71 feet. In 1942 the R-2800-41 Pratt & Whitney engines were introduced, which developed 2000 horsepower for takeoff. The B-26 Marauder design with its cigar-shaped circular fuselage, its wing loading, and its landing speed of 130 mph, was ahead of its time. The B-26 proved itself in combat with its ability to fly daylight missions, destroy targets, sustain a great deal of damage, and return to base. I believed myself fortunate to have been assigned to fly the B-26 Marauder rather than the four-engine bombers that I had requested on completion of advanced-flying school.

A number of derogatory nicknames were assigned to the B-26 Marauder including "Flying Coffin," "Coffin Without Handles," and the "B-Dash Crash." As previously noted, the slogan was developed, "One a day in Tampa Bay." There was some justification. The B-26 was responsible for many deaths in training accidents and there were many in-flight emergencies. As a result of these problems there was a series of investigations. The Truman Committee recommended suspension of production. The Glenn L. Martin Co. and the military services investigated; one investigation was headed by General "Tooey" Spaatz, who became the first U.S. Air Force Chief of Staff. In 1942, General H.H. Arnold, commanding general of the Army Air Force, directed General James Doolittle to investigate the situation personally. The accidents were determined to be a result of inexperienced pilots and inexperienced maintenance mechanics, and of overloading the plane beyond the weight at which it could fly on one engine.

Early models of the B-26 aircraft were sent to the British in October 1941 and they were named Marauders by the Royal Air Force (RAF). The USAAF adopted the name. The Free French Air Force in North Africa was equipped with B-26s in 1943. Five squadrons of the South African Air Force, SAAF, were equipped with B-26s, in late 1943 and 1944, the first aircraft going to Libya. Marauders made history in the Mediterranean under General Doolittle flying strafing missions and doing low-level bombing, but their losses were high. The plane was also used in the Pacific, but for low-level and not the medium bombardment for which it was designed. The B-26 was eventually replaced in the Pacific by the Mitchell B-25, named for the air pioneer, Billy Mitchell.

In Europe the first two Marauder missions were flown at low level. The target was the Velsen generating station at Ijmuiden, Holland where the German submarine-pens were located. On the first mission on May 14, 1943, two planes were damaged and one pilot was killed. The time-delay fuses that were used allowed the Dutch workers to escape before the bombs detonated, which was their purpose, but they also permitted the Germans to disarm or remove them before appreciable damaged occurred.

The second low-level mission was scheduled for May 17, 1943. This scheduling was despite the extreme danger and the objection of the Marauder group's officers. Of the eleven aircraft that were sent on the second mission, only one, which had aborted the mission due to electrical failure, returned. The lead plane was brought down by flak. A midair collision brought down two planes after one received a direct hit and they collided. Three other planes were brought down by flak. On the return flight, the four remaining planes were shot down by German ME 109s.

After this tragic beginning, B-26 operations were temporarily discontinued and then followed by intensive training at medium altitudes after Norden precision bombsights had been installed in the aircraft.

Action was resumed on July 16, 1943, two months after the second Velsen mission. Flying at medium altitude, the 323rd Bomb Group successfully attacked the marshalling yards at Abbeville in northeastern France. In August 1943, the Eighth Air Force announced that all medium bombardment missions from England to Western Europe since May had been flown by B-26 Marauders. The Marauders were transferred to the 9th Air Force, which in 1944 was brought up to full strength. The 344th Bombardment Group became operational on March 6, 1944.

Scheduling

As pilots in the 344th Bomb Group our primary task was to fly bombing missions against targets on the European continent. Targets were assigned by the 9th Air Force to the 9th Bombardment Division and in turn to the 99th Wing (and also to the 97th and 98th Wings) and then to the bomb groups. Pilots had to be available to fly when scheduled, but when we were not scheduled we had relative freedom. Flight schedules were made by the squadron operations officer and posted in advance.

The crews were on standby when they were scheduled to fly. When the group was assigned a target the crews typically would be awakened at three or four in the morning. After breakfast, we reported for an operations briefing on the mission, the target and the weather. An intelligence briefing provided information regarding the target, and an estimate as to where enemy fighters and anti-aircraft fire (flak) might be encountered. The target areas were the most heavily defended by AA, with the more valuable target sites the most heavily protected.

Flying the Sortie

The typical mission, or sortie — a single flight of an airplane on a combat mission — was flown at an altitude of 10,000 to 12,000 feet. We flew without oxygen, which at that altitude was fatiguing. The flight time from our base in Britain to the target on the continent and return usually was three to four hours. The elapsed time, however, from getting up, pedaling to breakfast and to the flight line, being briefed, waiting for takeoff, flying to and from the target area, getting debriefed and pedaling back to the hut was most of the day. Often there were mission delays for weather, either local or at the target, or for other reasons. Sometimes a mission would be canceled, or "scrubbed," for reasons unknown to us. This could be disheartening after getting up at 3:00 A.M. and waiting around for a good part of the day.

After the briefing we would wait on the flight line until it was time to start engines. If a rough mission was anticipated, we might be a bit nervous, but after starting engines we were too busy to think about anything but the task at hand. At briefing we were provided with a document classified secret that showed the names of the pilots and position in the formation of each of the 36 aircraft. It also showed the time for starting engines, taxiing and takeoff and the time over certain points, for instance English coast out, enemy coast in, IP (initial point, or start of bomb run) time over target, enemy coast out, English coast in and base. The back page of the document had the radio call signs for the Boxes (Box 1 of 18 planes and Box 2 of 18 planes), fighter escort, Bomber Command, emergency homing, colors of the day and authenticators. These items of information were extremely important.

Everything we did was planned and precise. From the takeoff to joining in formation each action or movement was choreographed so that each plane could arrive in the proper slot at the proper time. Forming the group was hazardous at night or when visibility was low, as it was most of the time. Flying en route to the target was usually uneventful other than for aircraft malfunction, which was rare. If the mission was anticipated to be a rough one, there was apprehension. On occasion a few German Luftwaffe fighters would be sighted. Usually all was well until we neared the target and the formation was in range of German antiaircraft guns.

On arrival at the IP, we headed for the target. We could take evasive action, random turns to the right or left, but for the last minute or so of the bomb run, the plane had to be flown straight and level to enable the bombardier to line up the bombsight on the target and to release the bombs. During the bomb run the AA gun crews had their greatest opportunity for a kill.

The return flight from the target was different than flying en route. Returning to base we felt relieved from the pressure and pleased if we had bombed the target, although it wasn't possible to know the full extent of damage until the films were developed. If the aircraft had sustained damage or lost an engine it was sometimes a struggle to return to base, and then we had to sweat out the landing.

After returning from a mission we were scheduled for debriefing. At debriefing we were questioned about the target, the estimated damage to the target, bombs dropped, effectiveness of the AA defense, where we encountered AA fire, enemy aircraft and so on. We liked debriefing because we were given a ration of alcohol beforehand. Liquor was provided for relaxation, to make it easier for the crews to talk, but we enjoyed the effect as we did being on center stage and being asked for an opinion.

The sad part of the return from a mission was counting missing aircraft. From many missions all the planes returned. From others, the losses were heavy. The ground crews who maintained the aircraft were an extremely important part of the whole and generally underappreciated, although not by the pilots. Ground crews naturally developed an intense interest in the aircraft and the aircrews and felt really lost when a plane that they maintained failed to return. The aircrews regretted losing friends.

It might seem unimportant to talk about a dog, but for me as a dog lover, this story is poignant and still sad to relate. One of the flight-crew members, whom I didn't know but often saw on the flight line, had a German shepherd dog who was very faithful to him. The dog accompanied his master everywhere, and when the master went on a mission, the dog waited patiently but intently on the flight line for his return. One day the master failed to return. The dog waited at the flight line for several days, refusing attention from anyone and refusing food. Finally it seemed as though he had decided that his master wasn't coming back. The dog left the flight line, walked in front of a truck and was killed. This dog was smart, and although grief may have made him less alert, I think his action was deliberate.

A difficult thing for me was facing an empty bunk in the hut after the man who had occupied it was lost on a mission. The empty bunk represented so much — a lost aircraft, a lost friend, a lost life and unhappiness for many people who were related to or who knew the man. Usually the word would get around the squadron as to the observations of other crews when a plane was shot down. However, even if chutes had been seen we still wouldn't know whether the missing had been captured or if they had been shot while coming down in their chutes.

When I saw the stage play *Les Miserables* I was especially touched by the song "Empty Chairs and Empty Tables." It effectively summarized my feelings at that time and even now many years later.

Targets

The objectives of the medium-bombardment aircraft prior to D Day were to stop the Luftwaffe from flying by bombing airfields and destroying aircraft; to interdict and impede the movement of men and materiel to the coastal areas of France, to disrupt the transportation system and to destroy the launching sites in use or under construction for the pilotless V-1 or Buzz Bombs. The targets for the 344th Bomb Group included airfields, marshalling yards, railway facilities, coastal gun batteries, "noball" or pilotless-aircraft sites, and railway and highway bridges.

After D Day the Group struck gun positions, marshalling yards, choke points, fuel dumps, supply and ordnance depots, oil storage and repair depots, troop concentrations, and defended towns and positions. We continued striking railroad bridges, to isolate the German forces and interdict movement.

Combat

My first combat sortie was flown on March 7, 1944, less than five months after completing pilot training and being awarded my wings at Waco, in October 1943. What a different world! After a pleasant drive from Texas to Florida, two months in Lakeland and Savannah, and a long flight, including a short "vacation" in Marrakech, I was in Britain and in combat.

As a teenager when the war began in Europe, I remember discussing with my friends whether the United States was likely to get involved in the war: we believed it would. On active duty with the Army, I was training for war. After being trained for combat and subsequently training infantry units and recruits, and with the United States then involved in the war, I was afraid I would still be giving basic training when the war ended! That was one of my strong reasons for going in to the Air Corps (later the Army Air Force and, in 1947, the USAF). The primary reason was that I wanted to fly.

Gone With the Wind

I thought that the situation in Texas before the U.S. entry into the war seemed similar to the situation described in *Gone With the Wind*. Just before the Civil War, Scarlett O'Hara was entertaining the Tarleton twins and other friends at Tara and the young men were eagerly anticipating their involvement in the war. My friends and I also were patriotic and eager to be in service. No one whom I knew would have thought of evading military service; it was a matter of honor to participate. Similarly, after the war was over, the life that we had known before the war was gone.

The Last 'Great' War

World War II was different from the military engagements the United States subsequently became involved in. Our country had been attacked; we had a common enemy, and the public supported U.S. involvement and the military forces. Then it was exhilarating to be a pilot, to be in Europe and to be a part of a force fighting against what we perceived as the enemy. The war created a sense of urgency and of excitement. All relationships were heightened because we could not know when we said good-bye whether it would be the last time. Never did I dwell on that thought or believe I would be killed, but there was a poignancy to things said and done and especially to partings.

I was glad to be in Europe and in combat because I believed I was contributing to the end of the war and to the preservation of a way of life. We had seen and experienced in England the killing of many people and the destruction of buildings. We had heard descriptions of what had occurred in Germany and the German-occupied countries in Western Europe. In addition, the war had become very personal, as I was being shot at when in the air and bombs were dropping very close to me on the ground.

In a letter home of July 24, 1944, I wrote, "My radio gunner was on the British Broadcasting System, made a four-minute broadcast about a mission. I was flying first pilot and we had the right engine cut out on the bomb run but got it going again and came back with the formation. They got Sgt. Johnson to London to tell about it. Not that it amounted to anything, but they have to have something to broadcast. Charley got some publicity anyway. I think it was on the Coca Cola broadcast in the states — Sgt. Chas. H. Johnson, radio gunner of 'Six Hits and a Miss;' did you hear the broadcast?

"Our new plane is named 'Lili Marlene' after a song that is becoming popular now. It was started in North Africa and there is a story attached. Mrs. Hartley sent me a box of candy bars, Milky Ways and Butterfingers. Don't know anything for sure about when I'll get back, but I'm not complaining yet. Have 42 now (in five months). About to run out of news. Dreamt the other night that I was home and had a big Buick convertible. Hope it comes true soon." I was home about a year later, but it took two years for the Buick convertible.

The Flight Crew

Initially I flew as copilot with a captain, flight commander. After I was checked out as a first pilot I had my own crew. The flight crew consisted of me as pilot, the copilot, C.E. "Snuffy" Smith, the navigator—bombardier, Jack Cargill, aircraft engineer, Frank Cole, radio operator and waist gunner, Charles Johnson, armament man and turret gunner, Kenneth Bowman. The engineer was also tail gunner. Four 50-caliber machine guns were mounted on the front of the aircraft that were controlled by the pilot! I sought opportunity to fire the machine guns against enemy fighter aircraft, but opportunity came only twice, when we were attacked by Luftwaffe. The Luftwaffe had largely been destroyed in the air during the Battle of Britain, and on the ground with the bombing of the airfields so they were not much of a threat. At first we had fighter escort on some missions, but they were later dispensed with.

The crew: Back row, Jack Cargill, navigator—bombardier; C.E. "Snuffy" Smith, copilot; Bill Bauers (the author), pilot
Front row, Frank Cole, engineer, tail gunner; Charles Johnson, radio operator, waist gunner; Kenneth Bowman, turret gunner

Original crew with Captain Shimmin

111

Snuffy Smith was very quiet, perhaps a bit overwhelmed by the situation, and I never really got to know him. Cargill was always fun to be with: I enjoyed his company on the ground and in the air. Jack's predecessor, Harry Hague, was quiet, but also had a good sense of humor and enjoyed life. The enlisted crew were great. The relationship between the officers and enlisted men on flight crews was different from that between officers and enlisted men in the army. We were more informal. The crew called me Skipper or Lucky and we bantered on occasion, but they never crossed the line. They all came to Washington, D.C. for my wedding when I got married, which I very much appreciated.

Frank Cole, as tail gunner, was in the part of the aircraft that had the greatest motion, the tail. He told me one day that he got airsick on every mission. Nevertheless, he didn't let it interfere with his performance as a crew member and every day we were scheduled he went back up. It was an example of the courage and dedication to duty on the part of the crew. They were always confident and upbeat. At least that's how they presented themselves. When we started out they were a bit uncertain but later had complete confidence in my ability to get them back.

Flak

Antiaircraft fire, or flak, was a bigger threat than enemy aircraft. On one mission the turret gunner, Kenneth Bowman, had a piece of flak come through the Plexiglas of the turret. He picked it up and found the initials "KB" on it. "That's really getting too close," he exclaimed, "when you get a piece of flak with your initials on it!" There were other near misses and one occasion when the flak didn't miss.

Germany's heavy flak defenses, 80 percent of which were made up of "88s" protecting industrial targets, communication centers, bridges, and other targets, were capable of achieving deadly results by firing up to 20 rounds per minute. To supplement the 88 millimeter flak gun, there were static and mobile versions of a 105mm flak gun and a 128mm weapon and others. Railway-mounted heavy flak was used to rapidly reinforce threatened areas. The 88mm shells weighed 20 pounds; the 105mm and 128mm, respectively, weighed 33 and 57 pounds. The guns fired high explosive shells with time fuses that exploded at a predetermined altitude. Germany had an early-warning radar system to provide for the detection of hostile aircraft, which was most effective prior to the invasion of the continent.

Through the use of flak intelligence, every effort was made by the Ninth Bombardment Division to avoid known or suspected flak defenses in planning routes to the targets. Evasive action, such as planned definite but irregular turns, was used until the bomb run was started. Accuracy of bombing results required a straight and level bomb run of 45 to 60 seconds. After bombs away, a sharp turn and loss of altitude were standard procedure.

Countermeasures to neutralize flak included use of high-explosive and fragmentation bombs dropped by aircraft slightly ahead of the main formation, or strafing and bombing by fighter aircraft in a coordinated attack. Radio countermeasures were used when cloud cover existed to deny the use of radar for direction of the AA guns. Shredded aluminum, referred to as "window," was dropped to confuse the enemy radar. Socalled window aircraft, three per group, went ahead of the group about one mile and 1000 feet below the lead ship and dropped bundles of window, as did the group ships, with different frequencies and intensity, to reduce effective use of the enemy radar for range finding. (Flak Facts, 9th Air Force)

Milk Runs and Others

Some combat missions were considered "easy" — that is, they were a short run and/or there was a lack of or limited antiaircraft fire en route to or at the target. These sorties were called milk runs. Important targets were heavily guarded, and the flak crews were very accurate. They were able to gauge our direction, speed and altitude and to place the flak where we were rather than where we had been. If you have ever shot skeet or ducks, you know that when aiming you have to lead a moving target in order to hit it. The AA gun crews knew how to do it.

To flight crews, flak would appear to be small puffs of black smoke, like very small black clouds. Sometimes you could see the orange flame or hear the noise of the burst or the metal fragments hitting the metal of the aircraft. Seeing the flak bursts around you was disconcerting but it was the bursts that you didn't see that were often deadly. It was very disturbing to see an aircraft receive a direct hit. There was nothing you could do to help the crew. You could just imagine their agony and continue on to the target. If the crew members of the doomed plane had the opportunity to bail out we would try to count the number of chutes.

D Day

Early in the morning on June 6, 1944, flight crews of the 344th were awakened, and after midnight chow, they rode bicycles or weapons carriers to the briefing shack. The weather was poor for flying, dark, raining and windy, with low ceilings and visibility. The operations map was draped as usual with a green cloth. After everyone was seated, the briefing officer announced that this was D Day, the Allied invasion of the continent of Western Europe.

The targets for the 344th were three coastal batteries on the Cherbourg Peninsula on the beaches at Beau Guillot, La Madeleine and Martin de Varreville, to be struck just a few minutes before the ground troops were to hit the beach. These gun batteries had the power to sink ships, and it was imperative that they be knocked out. It had to be on the first pass; there would be no second time around.

Prior to June 6, only a handful of men had been briefed on what this date was to be — the group commander, the deputy commander, and group navigator and a few others. The night before, the ground crews were directed to paint special markings, black-and-white stripes on the aircraft wings and fuselage for identification as Allied planes.

The 54 aircraft of the 344th Bombardment Group were led by Lieutenant Colonel Robert Witty, the deputy group commander. The group led the Ninth Air Force and spearheaded the aircraft of the invasion force. Colonel Witty had been involved in the planning of the first raid over Tokyo and had volunteered for the mission, but to his disappointment did not get to go. He was grounded for two weeks prior to D Day to assure that he could go on this one.

At 0330 the planes were manned and at 0412 the first planes took off into a murky darkness, with cloud cover above and rain squalls restricting the altitude the 54 plane maximum effort could achieve. The bombs found their mark and silenced their targets

That afternoon, the second mission of the day went out, to strike the marshalling yard at Amiens. On June 5, the previous day, our mission was to hit the headquarters at Wissant, and on June 7, the following day, the marshalling yard at Argentan. I flew on both these missions but was disappointed that I missed the big one on the sixth. Crossing the channel

115

on the sixth and seventh there were more ships and landing craft than had ever before been assembled. Each plane and glider had been specially marked to indicate that it was part of the Allied forces. All were participating in this great effort, Operation Overlord, the invasion of the continent of Europe.

By June 27, Cherbourg fell to American troops. The Allied invasion moved on, winning victories, reaching Troyes, a railroad center, and Reims and liberating Paris. But it would be almost a year before the war ended.

Death in the Sky

On April 22, 1944, the second mission of the day, we attacked a construction site at Siracourt, a "Noball" site. The target was heavily defended by AA, typical of these sites. The aircraft flying to my right received a direct flak hit. I saw one crew member go out of the waist-gun window without a chute. (Two chutes were seen.) The cockpit quickly became engulfed in flames, and I could see the pilot surrounded by fire as the plane went down. He was a friend, as was the navigator. This was an image I am not likely to forget.

On another mission I was flying as first pilot, my wing man on the right received a direct hit in the left engine that made his plane veer suddenly and dramatically to the left, directly into mine. I pulled the elevator control back into my lap in order to pull the plane up and avoid a midair collision. And I prayed. The stricken plane sailed by under our plane. The crew said that it didn't miss us by more than a few feet.

During my combat tour many of our planes were shot down. On a mission to a target on the outskirts of Paris, five planes from our group were shot down by AA fire in what seemed a matter of seconds. It looked as though they were flies swatted from the sky by a giant flyswatter. This was one of the times when I was concerned. It was uncertain whether we would make it past the target.

Near Miss

No member of my crew was seriously wounded on board my aircraft but we did have near misses. One day I moved my seat forward a few inches to change position. Just after I did so, a piece of flak came through the fuselage and lodged in the framework of my seat just behind me, where my head would have been if I hadn't moved. On another occasion, I bent down to pick up a pencil I had dropped and just then a piece of flak came through the window, passing through the space I had just vacated. My crew nicknamed me "Lucky." Before that my nickname was "Curly." I liked "Lucky" better.

Loss of a Crew Member

The navigator—bombardier who started the tour with us, Harry Hague, who was also a good friend, became very restive after flying a number of missions. He was anxious to get home to his wife. Against my recommendation and counsel, he volunteered to fly additional missions with other crews so he could finish his tour and get home sooner. His luck ran out. The plane he was in one day was shot down, and as far as I know none of the crew survived. Had he stayed with us he would have been okay. This gives credence to the adage, Don't volunteer. I was very sorry Harry didn't make it. We were fellow survivors of a number of trips to London as well as a number of missions. His widow wrote to me seeking information but I didn't know what had happened.

Jack Cargill took Harry's position as navigator—bombardier and finished the tour with me. Jack had a great deal of joie de vivre and a good sense of humor. He also became a good friend. In France, when we were living in a shack on an abandoned airfield formerly occupied by the Germans, Jack would go around the French countryside scouting for food, swapping cigarettes for eggs and bread. We couldn't eat the alleged food that was slopped into our mess kits in the chow lines. (I never figured out how they could create green scrambled eggs). The loot that Jack brought back from his excursions and the packages from home helped us survive the war, though I was considerably lighter in weight than before, by about twenty pounds. Jack went back to California after the war, and we lost touch.

Formation

A flight consisted of six aircraft: the lead aircraft, and two wing men, one on either side of the lead, and the deputy lead and two wing men. The deputy lead flew directly behind the lead aircraft and slightly lower (the number-four position). The B-26s flew in very close formation to improve the bombing effectiveness. All the planes followed the lead plane, dropping their bombs at the same time. Close formation was indicated also to make us a smaller target for the AA guns, but sometimes I wondered if it didn't make it easier to hit us. The close formation enhanced our firepower against any fighters that chose to attack.

The bomb group ordinarily put up six flights for a mission, for a total of 36 aircraft from the four squadrons. The aircraft took off from the runway at 15-second intervals and joined in formation over the airfield. Assembling 36 aircraft required precise timing, a specific timed plan for joining formation and a great deal of skill, plus a strong nervous system. Two planes would take the runway at the same time. The engines were revved up, brought almost to full power, with the brakes on. At the precise second, the pilot released the brakes and applied full power. Fifteen seconds later, the second aircraft would start the takeoff roll, and two more planes would take the runway. It was all carefully choreographed.

One day the plane ahead of me aborted on takeoff and was about mid-runway when it was time for my plane to roll. My thought was that if I didn't go ahead, everyone else's timing would be screwed up. If I did let the plane roll it was likely that the other aircraft would be far enough down the runway to be out of the way, so I made the instant decision to roll! When I talked to the guys who had been on the ground, they said they were holding their breath.

The typical weather in England and the usual lack of visibility made the task of forming the group of 36 planes difficult and dangerous. I remember the day, March 8, 1944, the group's third mission, target Soesterberg, there was a midair collision of two aircraft while joining the formation in restricted visibility, killing the crews of both, twelve airmen, including my good friend, Johnny Eckert. I also remember the funeral held a few days later for all twelve and their burial, in a cemetary near the base in a common grave. It was a gut wrenching experience.

Death in the Afternoon

Another incident hit me very hard. It was on August 25, 1944, prior to a mission to Brest, that I had lunch with a fellow pilot just before we were to take off. We had been briefed and were ready to go when the mission was delayed, so we were given time for lunch. A half-hour after lunch he was dead. I can still see his face but I can't remember his name. I guess I've blocked it out. He was young, about 22, handsome, a great guy, a friend. He was killed along with another pilot, Bill Geary, who also was a good friend. On takeoff their aircraft lost an engine. With a full load of fuel and a bomb load of 4,000 pounds, they could not maintain flight and did not survive the crash. They had taken off shortly before I did, and I flew over the crash site as I took off. It was a devastating day.

That evening I went to the officers' club with the goal of blotting the event out of my mind. I ordered a double scotch, followed by a double vodka. As I recall, I had four drinks, two of each, before leaving the club. About halfway back to my Nissen hut I passed out. I woke up later lying on the ground with rain beating down on me. I made it back to the hut and then got sick. The next day I felt awful for two reasons rather than one. I realized that the way I handled the situation wasn't the way to do it, but I didn't know any other way. It was tough trying to handle the hurt. You couldn't show emotion, you couldn't cry. You just went on, and after a while you became somewhat inured to the pain. Many of my friends were killed, or they were shot down and I didn't know the outcome. Censorship prevented our writing to the families. The theory was that if a letter were to be intercepted, it could give aid and comfort to the enemy. I never accepted the theory but had to live with it.

The Survivor

I thought that after the war I would visit the widows or parents of my friends to tell them what I knew and to express my sympathy. But when I returned to the United States my thinking was that a visit from a stranger probably wouldn't help and that the families might resent the fact that I had survived and their husband or son didn't. Perhaps I felt guilty in having made it back. Some of the guys I knew were terrific human beings who deserved to live, but didn't get the chance. I couldn't understand why they had to die, and the chaplain couldn't explain it to me. I still wonder. After it was over I was ready to forget the war and go on with my life. But the war never went away, details have gone away but the experiences are indelibly imprinted.

The B-26s in the European Theater had a calculated loss rate of less than 1 percent, officially about one half of 1 percent, which was touted as being extremely low, and it was. I calculated, however, that if the group flew 200 missions, based on a one-half percent loss rate, the group would be wiped out. As we were required to fly a combat tour of 65 missions, the odds of survival were good but not entirely in our favor. The 344th completed 200 missions in less than a year; the group was operational on March 6, 1944, and had completed 200 missions by February 14, 1945. The B-26 could take a lot of punishment and I must have had a guardian angel, but there were a few times when it was touch-and-go.

Silver Star Day

Our mission one particular day was difficult. Flak was intense, and our flight was the last flight over the target. I was flying as first pilot, deputy lead, in the number-four position. The lead plane was hit by flak and dropped out of formation. Immediately I took over the flight lead, pulling up into the number-one position as lead aircraft. On the bomb run the target was obscured by smoke from the bombs dropped by the flights ahead of us, and the bombardier could not see the target in the bombsight. From what we could see, it did not appear that the target had been destroyed, and we had a load of bombs. I made the decision to go around and to make another bomb run. Of course, by that time the flak guns had zeroed in on us. They knew our speed and altitude and we were sitting ducks as the only flight of aircraft remaining in the area. On the bomb run the plane had to be flown straight and level long enough for the bombardier to line up the bombsight with the target, at which time we were most vulnerable. I knew that we would be in grave danger the second time around. Flak hit the nose of the aircraft, the greenhouse, the bombardier's position, shattering the Plexiglass and injuring Jack, the bombardier. After we made a quick assessment, Jack and I elected to continue the bomb run. As soon as the bombs were dropped, I pushed the nose of the aircraft down to lose altitude and gain speed, to get the hell out of the area and out of range of the AA guns.

On the return flight to the U.K. as five lone aircraft, we were attacked by a couple of enemy fighters but when we opened fire with 50-caliber tracer bullets they didn't stay around long. Upon preparing to land at the base we discovered that the nose gear had been disabled by the flak that hit the plane. The nose wheel had been shot off. I ordered the crew to move everything that was loose to the rear of the plane, including themselves, to keep the weight off the nose. With tricycle landing gear the B-26 landed on the main gear and as the plane slowed, the nose gear would be lowered to the ground. For this landing I held the nose of the plane off the ground as long as possible. When the nose went forward the strut held, so there was no further damage to the plane. We were met by an ambulance and fire trucks, which provided a bit of additional excitement.

The squadron operations officer heard about what had occurred. He called me in and said that he wanted to recommend both the bombardier and me for the Silver Star, a medal for "gallantry in action." It was a medal I coveted. He told us to write the citations, and he would submit them. I didn't think it was appropriate for me to write my own citation, so I didn't. Jack didn't have such qualms. He was awarded the Silver Star, as well as the Purple Heart for being wounded in action.

Dropping Out

We often had to ascend through clouds to get to altitude or fly at least part of the mission under instrument conditions. The group had one squadron commander who when he flew the group lead was all over the sky. It is essential for the lead pilot of a formation to hold the aircraft steady, especially when flying on instruments, otherwise it is extremely difficult for the pilots who fly the wing positions, especially the left wing position. I was flying a mission on his left wing under instrument conditions! Suddenly the lead dropped the left wing of his plane and headed toward me. I had to pull out of formation into the "soup" to avoid a midair collision. After pulling out I could not then see the formation and had to start flying on instruments immediately. That is a difficult adjustment to make quickly, and it is easy to get disoriented. The navigator had to determine our position, and we continued on toward the target, alone. Because of the weather we dropped down to a low altitude, returning across the English Channel. Getting near the southern coast of England, I suddenly realized we were about to fly into a balloon barrage. These were steel cables attached to the ground at one end and to balloons at the other. They were designed to sever the wings of aircraft flying into them — an air defense device. We maneuvered around the balloons and were late getting back to base. The operations officer razzed me and said that he was going to get me a seeing-eye dog to put in the nose of my plane so I could follow the formation.

Trading Places

Initially I flew as copilot for a flight commander, as part of his crew, because I had not had the opportunity to go through transition training for the B-26. In Britain generally it wasn't possible to fly for training because of the shortage of fuel and the need to preserve the aircraft for missions. There were few training flights.

As I was flying with a flight leader, I wasn't able to get practice in formation flying. It was important for me to learn to fly formation well and I liked it. Flying close formation required a very delicate touch on the throttles and on the controls and the ability to anticipate the need for increased or reduced power in order to get into position and to remain there. One morning, while the crews were on the flight line waiting for the designated time to start engines, Johnny Dye came over to me and said, "Why don't we trade places today? You can fly as a wing man and get some practice in formation flying." I recalled what Johnny had said to me in Savannah about not coming back, and my initial reaction was to say no. But then I thought, *"This is silly!"* So I answered "Sure, Johnny, thanks! I'd like to do that."

That day Johnny was shot down and killed, flying in the plane I would have been in had we not traded places. I felt really bad about his death, and thought that in a way I was responsible for it. But then I thought, if I had flown in the aircraft as originally scheduled, I wouldn't have been at exactly the same spot at the exact time he was. Perhaps it was his time to go. I wondered if he had precognition back in Savannah, or if his thinking had set up the situation causing his death. I was grateful I was still around, but really sorry about Johnny. The event caused me to ponder God, fate and chance. Life hangs on a slender thread.

On another day I had been scheduled to fly as copilot with Captain Harvey Johnson, but discovered that I also was scheduled to be officer of the day (OD). So I went to see the squadron operations officer and said, "I can't be in two places at the same time; which would you prefer that I do?" His response was, "Why don't you take OD and I'll get someone else to fly with Harvey." That day Harvey's plane was shot down, and I didn't know what happened to the crew.

After the war I was back in San Antonio and my sister said, "We met a former B-26 pilot, and he wants to meet you. He was in your group." I didn't recognize the name. The introduction was arranged, and the pilot and I played 20 questions. I did not remember him but learned that we had been in the same squadron! I couldn't understand why I didn't know him. He said, "Well, I came into the squadron as a replacement pilot and had just arrived at Stansted. I had been there just one day, and I was assigned to fly with Harvey Johnson. We were shot down on my first mission! We bailed out! We were captured and spent the rest of the war as POWs." I said, "Thanks a lot! I really appreciate what you did for me!"

Harvey Johnson, you may recall, in 1943 had to ditch in the Atlantic en route to Roberts Field, Liberia. Leaving Ascension Island, he crashed, losing his entire crew. After flying a number of combat missions, he was shot down on April 20, 1944, and completed the war as a POW, as did Johnny Guiher and Jack Porter. Thanks to Cletus Wray's decision that I should be OD, I was not flying with Harvey that day. Johnny Guiher, who had been with Cletus Wray when he ditched in the Atlantic, was with Harvey Johnson when he was shot down, as was Jack Porter, the copilot, who was flying in my stead.

Fire Aboard

Returning from a mission, we were almost ready to land when a dangerous incident occurred. The engineer usually stood in the passageway between the pilot and copilot seats to observe the gauges and what was going on. He accidentally knocked the flare gun that was carried for emergencies out of its holder. It hit the deck and fired a flare, which pierced a hydraulic line and set the fluid on fire. The fire spread, and smoke filled the cockpit. We couldn't see but refrained from opening a window to avoid fanning the flames. The engineer quickly grabbed a fire extinguisher and extinguished the flames. Without hydraulic fluid, we had to crank the landing gear down to lower it into place. Again, we were very lucky. A similar incident in another squadron with the plane on the ground resulted in the death of the pilot and serious injury to the copilot.

Author's Note

After my combat tour was completed, I made a list of the combat missions I had flown from data maintained by the squadron operations officer (see appendix). The data indicated the date, morning or afternoon if two missions were flown on one day, the location of the target, the type of target and the results of the bombing effort based on aerial photos taken.

Missions noted as "Pathfinder," or "PFF," were those missions led by especially trained crews from a Pathfinder squadron. They used OBOE to locate the target and drop the bombs when the target was obscured due to weather. On Pathfinder missions there were no photos taken, so results were not available until later, through intelligence reports. Those targets designated "Noball" were V-1 or V-2 launching sites.

The OBOE system was developed and maintained by the RAF, as it was a British invention. At that time the system was classified, and we knew nothing about its operation except that we were to follow the Pathfinder lead. OBOE used a pattern of audio signals and lights to inform the Pathfinder pilot and bombardier when the plane was on course, when to open the bomb-bay doors and when to drop. Precision flying was required. The time of arrival at the IP had to be within one minute of the scheduled time in order to receive the OBOE signal, which came from the ground. The system had great accuracy and enabled striking a target without visual sighting.

GO 109

GENERAL ORDERS }   WAR DEPARTMENT
No. 109   WASHINGTON 25, D. C., 24 November 1945

    BATTLE HONORS.—As authorized by Executive Order 9396 (sec. I, WD Bul. 22, 1943), superseding Executive Order 9075 (sec. III, WD Bul. 11, 1942), citations of the following units in the general orders indicated are confirmed under the provisions of section IV, WD Circular 333, 1943, in the name of the President of the United States as public evidence of deserved honor and distinction. The citations read as follows:

    11. The *344th Bombardment Group (M)* is cited for extraordinary heroism in armed conflict with the enemy from 24–26 July 1944. The *344th Bombardment Group (M)* played a vital role in preparing the way for an Allied offensive on the Cherbourg Peninsula by attacking four vital enemy installations. On 24 July the group dispatched 39 aircraft to attack a key bridge over the Loira River near Tours, which was being used to bring hostile reinforcements into the St. Lo sector. Despite an intense barrage of antiaircraft fire which dispersed the lead flight and damaged 31 aircraft, the intrepid airmen dispatched their bombs with telling effect and destroyed the bridge. On the morning of the following day a full-strength attack was launched against enemy troop concentrations in the path of Allied troops advancing in the area of St. Lo. Four hours later the group attacked and severed a railroad viaduct at Maintenon, and, on 26 July, a formation of B-26 type aircraft from the group destroyed a large supply of fuel and ammunition. As a result of the gallant courage of the airmen and the determined efforts of the ground personnel, the Allied ground forces were able to advance over the area with minimum losses. By their bravery and determination, the officers and men of the *344th Bombardment Group (M)* reflect great credit on themselves and the Army Air Forces. (General Orders 170, Headquarters Ninth Air Force, 31 August 1945, as approved by the Commanding General, European Theater (Main).)

Award of Presidential Unit Citation
(Excerpt from General Order No. 109)

Six hits and a miss, Johnny Catlin in the cockpit

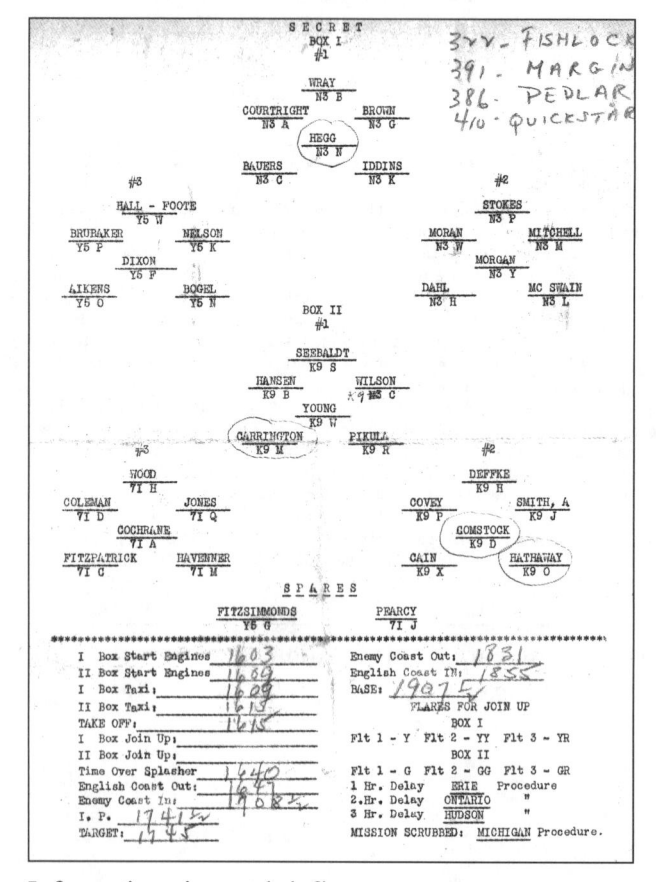

```
                    S E C R E T
                       BOX I
                        #1                    3YY - FISHLOCK
                       WRAY                   391 - MARGIN
                       N3 B                   386 - PEDLAR
          COURTRIGHT        BROWN             4/0 - QUICKSTAR
            N3 A            N3 G
                       HEGG
                       N3 N
            BAUERS          IDDINS
            N3 C            N3 K
    #3                                              #2
                                          STOKES
    HALL - FOOTE                          N3 P
       Y5 W
 BRUBAKER    NELSON                  MORAN      MITCHELL
   Y5 P      Y5 K                    N3 W        N3 M
         DIXON                           MORGAN
         Y5 F                            N3 Y
  AIKENS     BOGEL                   DAHL       MC SWAIN
   Y5 O     Y5 N                     N3 H        N3 L
                       BOX II
                        #1
                      SEEBALDT
                        K9 S
             HANSEN         WILSON
              K9 B           K9 C
                       YOUNG
                       K9 W
           CARRINGTON       PIKULA
              K9 M           K9 R
    #3                                              #2
                                         DEFFKE
           WOOD                           K9 B
           71 H
  COLEMAN     JONES                  COVEY       SMITH, A
   71 D       71 Q                   K9 P         K9 J
         COCHRANE                         COMSTOCK
          71 A                             K9 D
 FITZPATRICK  HAVENNER               CAIN        HATHAWAY
   71 C       71 M                   K9 X         K9 O
                    S P A R E S
              FITZSIMMONDS    PEARCY
                 Y5 G          71 J
**********************************************************
I  Box Start Engines 1603    Enemy Coast Out: 1831
II Box Start Engines 1609    English Coast In: 1855
I  Box Taxi:         1609    BASE: 1907½
II Box Taxi:         1613           FLARES FOR JOIN UP
TAKE OFF:            1615                 BOX I
I  Box Join Up:              Flt 1 - Y  Flt 2 - YY  Flt 3 - YR
II Box Join Up:                           BOX II
Time Over Splasher   1640    Flt 1 - G  Flt 2 - GG  Flt 3 - GR
English Coast Out:   1649    1 Hr. Delay  ERIE   Procedure
Enemy Coast In:      1708½   2. Hr. Delay ONTARIO    "
I. P.                1741½   3 Hr. Delay  HUDSON     "
TARGET:              1745    MISSION SCRUBBED: MICHIGAN Procedure.
```

Information given at briefing

CHAPTER TEN

ON THE CONTINENT

France in the Fall

In the fall of 1944, a few months after D Day, after our forces had advanced in Europe and Paris was liberated, the 344th Bomb Group was transferred to an airfield near Cormeilles-en-Vexin in France. The Germans had abandoned the airfield when they retreated from the advancing Allied forces. What had not been destroyed by Allied bombing, the retreating Germans blew up. Few buildings were still standing. Gone was the good life that we had at Stansted. In France we had tents to live in, outdoor latrines and no bathing facilities.

When the announcement was made that the group was being transferred to France, we were sworn to secrecy and restricted to the base. Later in a letter from Sylvia, the young model and cover girl in Stansted, I learned that the people in town suspected something was afoot, because there weren't any fliers in the pubs. That evening of the announcement I had planned to see Sylvia, but I could neither leave the base nor call her. After we had settled in France I wrote to tell her what happened but didn't see her again.

Home Is Where You Find It

My bombardier, Jack, and I found the remnants of an abandoned building on the base and moved in, preferring it to a tent. One small room remained in which there were crudely made wood bunk beds. That room became our home away from home. The bunk beds had only the wooden slats remaining. There were no mattresses, and we couldn't have used them had they been left. Wood slats and a blanket were what I slept on for months. It was less than comfortable and I often wished that my bedroll could be retrieved from the Sahara, but that was not to be. In contrast to life in England, this was a miserable existence, with cold and rainy weather that fall and winter. The only compensation was that the targets were closer to our base and thus the missions were shorter.

If I could ever sleep on clean sheets again and have a telephone, my life, I thought, would be complete. I don't know why the telephone seemed important, other than as a symbol of civilized life. Most things previously considered important were not important. In a wartime situation, it did not matter whether your family had money or social position or how you lived before. What you were and the friends you had were the only things that mattered at the moment.

Looking Back

Before going into combat I wondered what my reaction would be in life-threatening situations. Would I be afraid? Facing danger proved not to be a problem for me, because of the faith I had in the outcome, and the belief that someone was looking out for me. I also believed in what we were doing and enjoyed life much of the time. The loss of friends was the hard part. My performance measured up. Luckily I finished my combat tour of 68 missions with my integrity and my crew intact and without injury.

A Mess

Food on the continent was served in an outdoor mess line. We had to stand in line, usually in the rain, with a mess kit, a metal container with a handle developed by the Army to be carried in a backpack. The food was lined up on tables and unceremoniously slopped into the mess kits by the servers as the men moved down the line. There were no compartments in the mess kit, so everything ran together. It was aptly named: It was a mess. As if that were not enough to kill your appetite, the scrambled eggs for breakfast and the liver served for dinner were green! How that green color was achieved I don't know. The fallout was that often I just did not bother to eat except for what Jack scrounged from the French farmers in the countryside in exchange for our cigarettes, and packages from home.

Parlez Francais S'il Vous Plait

While we were in France there were a few incidents on the base that suggested attempted sabotage of the aircraft. To avoid a recurrence, the order was issued that no one other than American military personnel was allowed on the base without authorization. As there were no fences and few guards, the order was difficult to enforce.

One morning a group of us were standing around having a discussion when we saw a small farmer with a donkey cart coming across the field. Lieutenant Colonel Del Bentley, the 497th Squadron commander, said, "I speak French, I'll tell him he can't cross here." Bentley was a dynamic officer from Wyoming who always wore cowboy boots and in other ways was a bit of a maverick, but was very likable and a superb pilot. Walking over to the farmer, Bentley spoke to him in his best French. The farmer replied "Je ne parle pas Anglais, parlez francais, s'il vous plait." Bentley exploded, "I am speaking French, you dumb son of a bitch!" Not comprehending, the farmer continued on his way across the field, while the rest of us doubled up laughing.

I Loved Paris

The best part of the war was the occasional 48-hour pass to Paris. I loved Paris! Of course I visited Notre Dame Cathedral, Napoleon's tomb, and Montmarte. The shows at the Folies Bergère and some of the nightclubs, like the Moulin Rouge, were fantastic. The sidewalk cafes, especially on the Rue de la Paix, provided a delightful way to spend free time, or to relax, observing the passing parade, drinking coffee or aperitifs. It was hard to believe that the war was still very much with us. In Paris the war didn't exist. Paris had been declared an open city and thus had been spared from destruction, although as the Germans retreated, Hitler ordered that Paris be burned. Fortunately his officers did not follow this order. Paris is a beautiful city.

The Americans in Paris had a good time, and it seemed that most of the Parisians were enjoying themselves. They knew how to enjoy themselves and how to prepare food. They could make even K-rations taste delicious.

Sixty-Eight Accredited Combat Missions

On November 19, 1944, I flew my last combat mission. It was a rough one, almost literally my last. It was a Pathfinder mission; the weather obscured the target. The Pathfinder aircraft were equipped to locate a target using OBOE. Pathfinders led the group, and we bombed off their lead. Although we couldn't see the target, the AA could locate us. One of the aircraft engines ceased to function and we had to drop out of the formation and return to base alone. Operations advised me after my return to base that my combat tour was finished, with 68 accredited missions. They had just finished the calculations. I had actually flown 63 combat missions and expected to fly two more, but we were given dual credit for lead missions. Thus I had 68 missions accredited; I had 227 hours of combat time.

The Distinguished Flying Cross, (DFC), presented by Major General Andersen, the Air Medal with eleven oak leaf clusters (twelve air medals) and the European Theater ribbon with six oak leaf clusters had been awarded to me. The 344th Bombardment Group was awarded a Presidential Unit Citation "for extraordinary heroism in armed conflict with the enemy," and I was privileged to wear the blue ribbon representing it on the right pocket of my uniform.

No Second Tour

I did not want to leave the group to return to the States while the war continued in Europe, so I volunteered to fly a second combat tour. Operations advised that a second tour was not permissible, according to the existing policy. Some pilots had flown second tours, but it was found that their performance was affected and there were too many losses. Often their luck ran out.

My next request, if I couldn't fly combat, was to be assigned as squadron executive officer, a major's billet, a position that was open at the time and for which I was qualified. As that position called for a nonrated officer, however, the answer again was no. No reason; just policy.

On to 9th Bombardment Division Headquarters

Colonel Vance, the group commander, knew that I wanted an Air Force career and felt I should gain staff experience. On his recommendation, orders were issued assigning me to the 9th Bombardment Division Headquarters, Operations. The Headquarters was then located at Reims, France, which was familiar to me because at my parent's home in San Antonio there was a picture of the Cathedral at Reims hanging in the hall near the telephone stand.

I wrote home to say "I can't tell you where I am, but I could throw a rock at the building shown in the picture in the hall." My mother responded in her next letter, "You must have thrown a rock, because while I was talking to a friend on the telephone, the picture fell off the wall!"

When I started working at Headquarters it was quite difficult to adjust to sitting at a desk after the excitement of combat and the comradery of the squadron. In 9th Bomb Division Operations we planned and operated the missions assigned to the division. We had certain targets to hit, and based upon the assigned priorities, intelligence and weather, we selected the targets and the routing. The route was planned based on intelligence reports of the location of AA guns en route and at the target. My combat experience was helpful, and I tried to keep the aircrew perspective in mind.

The Operations section assigned the missions to the three wings and they in turn assigned targets to the groups. I came to know the three wing operations officers well and developed friendships by telephone although I never met them. Much of the time we were really busy, but there were intervals when nothing was happening. It was the quiet time that was difficult. There was time to think, and I thought of the pilots, my friends, who had been killed or wounded, and of the crews who would fly the missions we sent them on, and of the war and why it had become necessary.

My boss was Colonel John Reynolds, the division operations officer, whom I considered "old" at the time. Probably he was in his early forties. The Colonel always looked as if he knew something we didn't know, and I'm sure he did. He was easy to get along with as long as he didn't get riled, so we took care not to rile him and he let us do our job without interference. One day we had some quiet time, and I was reading the comics when Colonel Reynolds walked in. He said, "When I see someone reading comics, I feel that it indicates either a lack of intelligence, or a good sense of humor." I handed the newspaper to him, and said, "You read them, Colonel, and we'll determine which it is." Fortunately, he laughed and moved on.

The 9th Bomb Division Commander was Major General Samuel Anderson who was about 36 years old. He had early experience with the B-26 and had been involved in developing tactics, changing from low-level to medium-level daylight bombing, and improving bombing effectiveness. He was military in demeanor and intense, dapper, concerned about the Division and its record. We saw him rarely. His assistant, Lieutenant. Colonel Harold Moise was his liaison. Colonel Moise liked to come around and tell us stories about how things were when he was flying. General Richard Sanders was the chief of staff, one of the youngest generals in the service, a brigadier general at 27. After the war, while at the Pentagon, he broke his back and was retired for disability. Irony!

Shift Work

The operations desk where we worked had six telephones, providing direct contact with the 9th Air Force Headquarters and with the operations desks in the three Wings. The telephones could be silent at times and then all would ring at once. Theoretically we worked 8-hour shifts. There were three shifts, 8:00 A.M. to 4:00 P.M., 4:00 P.M. to midnight, and midnight to 8:00 A.M. These shifts were assigned for a week at a time; we worked seven days a week. If things were hot, we didn't leave when the shift was over. We often had fourteen-hour days, but it didn't matter, because we didn't have anywhere to go.

Claustrophobia

While the planes were in the air, we monitored the flights from a trailer equipped with communications facilities. We were obliged to be on duty in the trailer for hours at a time. Initially it was almost unbearable for me to be confined to the trailer. I felt like a caged bird. I went to

Colonel Reynolds to tell him I didn't think I could continue. He was understanding but suggested that I try it for a while longer. He promised to transfer me if I couldn't adjust. He was right, of course: I adjusted, and I stayed until the war in Europe ended.

I liked the work and found it fascinating. I preferred the 4:00 P.M.-to-midnight schedule. After getting off work I could get eight hours sleep and then have the day to do as I chose. The problem was that as soon as I got used to a schedule it was changed.

Jimmy Doolittle, Jr., was one of the officers assigned to Operations. Jimmy was over six feet tall, good-looking, smart, a good staff officer, and an excellent pilot, and I liked him (except when he laughed as I slipped and fell on the icy sidewalk outside headquarters.) It seemed that Jimmy had a great future in the Air Force. He said, however, that life in the Air Force as the son of a famous general was difficult for him. If he were promoted it was said to be because of his father; if he didn't, it was, "What's wrong with him?"

One afternoon General Doolittle was scheduled to land at our base, and Jimmy was advised of this so that he could be at the flight line. He invited me to go with him as I had expressed my desire to meet the general. Because of our work, at the operations desk, we were about fifteen minutes late. General Doolittle did not wait, but took off. Jimmy was disappointed and hurt. After the war Jimmy returned to Texas, and I was shocked to hear a couple of years later of his demise.

The WACs

For the first time in my career I worked with women who were called WACs, which stood for the Women's Army Corps. They were assigned work in the operations section and also operated the emergency communications trailer, which was next to the operations trailer. If a plane got into trouble the WACs, using two direction-finding stations to plot its location, could steer it to the nearest landing field, or if it was lost, orient the pilot and give him a heading to fly to return to base. On one occasion they failed to ask a pilot the altitude of his aircraft while giving the course to fly. Suddenly there was silence. We learned that the plane had flown into the side of a mountain. The young women were distraught. Although I tried to tell them that it wasn't their fault, they were inconsolable.

The WACs were capable and efficient and they brightened the landscape. Julie M. was stunning, a dark-haired beauty, who attracted a lot of unsolicited and unwanted attention. Another WAC was also a beauty and a lovely person. She, a sergeant, and a married Air Force lieutenant colonel became enamored of each other and spent a lot of time together despite the prohibition of officer-enlisted fraternization. They did a lot of hand-wringing and self-castigation, but couldn't resist the attraction. After the war, Jack went home, but shortly thereafter divorced his wife and married his wartime companion. Then there was Dorothy, from New York, who had short hair, always wore pants and smoked a pipe or cigars. She was a no-nonsense type and very efficient and did her job well.

I don't remember any of the others specifically but they deserve a lot of credit for doing an important job well in a difficult situation. I especially admired the women who worked in the emergency communications trailer. Every situation was a crisis; they handled it well because they were conscientious and knew what to do. The pilots liked hearing a woman's voice on the radio, and their voices carried well. They saved the lives of a number of crews.

A Not Very Merry Christmas

The invasion had succeeded and German forces had been pushed back from France and Belgium. Surprising many, however, they still had the strength to mount a major offensive, and on December 17, 1944, hit the American lines in the Ardennes with tank and infantry units driving a wedge in the lines. American troops were trapped at Bastogne. During this period, known as the Battle of the Bulge, fog and snow prevented the movement of our planes in support of the troops. Ninth Bomb Division Operations was under great pressure to get the planes in the air. Finally on December 23, the weather broke and a maximum effort was launched, with attacks against roads and railroads supplying the German offensive. It turned out to be a disastrous day for the B-26 Marauders, which were attacked by the Luftwaffe, with "41 aircraft lost, 166 battle damaged, 2 men killed, 227 missing, 30 wounded, and 2 injured." (John Moench, author of *Marauder Men*).

On Christmas Day Marauder forces flew without escort to knock out vital bridges. The 397th Bomb Group lost ten planes, and many others sustained battle damage. Working that day I felt terrible about these crews being shot down, killed or wounded, during Christmas week and particularly on Christmas day. As part of Division Operations I felt a measure of responsibility for sending them out, although I was part of the command chain and our efforts were essential to support the ground forces. For years after at Christmas I thought about that week and felt an almost overwhelming sadness.

Living Like the Addams Family

In Reims I had a room in a respectable building, but it had no heat. This seemed typical of my living quarters. I managed to get a kerosene heater that served its purpose satisfactorily except for the odor of kerosene. A major who was assigned as a temporary roommate failed to remember my warning about always turning off the heater when leaving the room, because if the heater ran out of kerosene, the wick burned. He went out one evening while I was working, leaving the heater burning. When I returned to the room after my shift, it looked like something out of a horror movie. The black smoke had left the room with an Addams family look. The room had what looked like black spiderwebs hanging from the walls and ceiling. Soot covered everything including the contents of the drawers and shelves. Everything had to be cleaned or laundered, and it took a long time for the odor to dissipate.

The Battle of the Bulge

During the Battle of the Bulge Germans were perilously near our area. We were prepared to evacuate if necessary. For protection, side arms, Colt 45 caliber pistols, were issued to the headquarters personnel, as German troops who spoke English and wore U.S. uniforms had parachuted into the area. The U.S. Army fought back and stopped the German offensive.

Belgium

The 9th Bomb Division Headquarters moved to Namur, Belgium, in 1945. We worked in a modern building, and I had the most attractive room that had been assigned to me during the war to date. Local Belgian women made the beds and cleaned the room. I had been studying French when I could, and in conversation I learned from one of the Belgian women that her husband and entire family had been killed by bombs and both their home and business had been destroyed. She had nothing. One day I had an orange left over from breakfast and gave it to her. She was so touched she cried.

R&R on the Riviera

In May 1945 I had a belated week of rest and recuperation at the Hotel Martinez in Cannes, on the French Riviera. I was supposed to have gone on R&R much earlier, after completing my combat tour, but my services were required at Headquarters, 9th Bombardment Division. Cannes was a touch of heaven. I had the opportunity to lie on the beach during the day and to party at night.

An Army nurse, Madge Paul, who was a close friend of my sister was by coincidence on the Riviera at the same time that I was. (It really was sheer coincidence.) Madge was a wonderful person, and it was good to see someone from San Antonio. She was very depressed because she had been working in an Army evacuation hospital, a ghastly place. Totally exhausted, Madge did not feel that she could return to the hospital.

On one occasion I had visited an evacuation hospital, and it was like descending into hell! There were men on stretchers lined up in the corridors waiting for medical attention, covered with blood, with terrible wounds, and missing arms and legs, some of them screaming in pain and others beyond feeling it.

VE Day

Fortunately, the War in Europe ended during the week that we were on the Riviera, on May 8, 1945. There was some jubilation at the Hotel Martinez but there wasn't a big celebration. The war had been too close to us and peace would neither cancel the devastation nor bring back the dead. We were glad the war was over. Some of the men became inebriated. For one chap, it proved to be the last time he would take a drink. Sliding down the banister in the hotel, he slipped off and fell several floors to his death on the lobby floor. That incident took the edge off any rejoicing. Furthermore, the war was still going on in the Pacific. It was highly probable that as pilots we would go there from Europe, via a leave in the States, but thanks to the atom bomb, the war in the Far East ended in August, after the bombing of Hiroshima and Nagasaki.

Waiting for Transportation

As we no longer had a purpose in Europe, it was time to go home. I was ordered to England to something that was akin to a concentration camp to await sea transport to the United States. The wait was more than a month, and it seemed much longer, like forever. It was difficult to decelerate from the activity and excitement of war to no activity. The camp was surrounded by a wire fence, and we were not allowed to leave except for an occasional pass. Some movies were shown but there was very little to do except think, which was not a good thing to do. The war seemed so wasteful. Many European cities had been destroyed, many civilians had been killed, and thousands of military men. Nurses along with Red Cross girls, including one who served us doughnuts and coffee at our base in France, were also killed.

Going Home

Ultimately I received orders to board a ship, the *S. S. Argentina*, along with a cast of thousands. I was surprised the ship didn't sink. Every available space on the ship was filled with hammock-type bunks, four or five to a tier. Sleeping on a hammock, it was impossible to roll over without bumping the guy above. The tiers were about a foot apart, if that. It was difficult to walk between them. I found the situation very tough to take. While wandering around the deck of the ship, I found a utility closet off the deck, with a port hole, and moved into it for the duration of the voyage. While not luxurious, and although I shared space with the brooms and mops, it was a cut above the hammocks.

No Promotion This Side of the Ocean

My promotion to major had been submitted for approval, but when the war had ended, all promotions were canceled. I was not sorry that the war ended, but did wish that the recommendation had been submitted a bit sooner. Major Sam Steere, with whom I worked at headquarters, had just been promoted. As a field officer (major and above), he had a cabin on upper deck.

Happy Fourth of July

Our ship docked in Norfolk, Virginia, on July 4, 1945, a very appropriate date. On arrival I was given orders to supervise a group of junior officers and enlisted men going to San Antonio, by rail. That was an assignment from hell. After returning from war and with the prospect of early release from the service, these guys cared not at all about military discipline or following orders, and they were in the mood to party. At every stop men were getting off the train, some going home by faster means, and those remaining on the train were whooping it up. Essentially because the group was uncontrollable but not doing any damage, I decided that the only thing I could do was go with the flow. I told the men getting off to be sure to report in San Antonio on the date we were expected to arrive, and they did.

A group of young, noncommissioned officers were doing a lot of celebrating on the train. One of the men asked me to have a drink with them. I said, "No thanks," and he reacted, "Why? Do you think that you're too good to drink with us, Captain?" The situation seemed like a no win, so I said,

"Okay. I'd be glad to have a drink with you." They were drinking Southern Comfort, which goes down very smoothly, like syrup. One sip followed another, and we had too good a time that evening. We celebrated the end of the war and going home! I was breaking the rules but occasionally they have to be broken. It was a good group of men who had fought valiantly. On arrival in San Antonio, with a hangover, I happily surrendered the group to the receiving organization. Then I went home by taxi from the railroad station.

Great Expectations

During the time that I was away I often thought about home and how great it would be to get back. Returning home was a letdown, perhaps because I anticipated too much and built up homecoming in my mind. It is also typical to have a letdown after a period of stress, and I had had almost five years of it. My parents were happy to see me and I was happy to see them, but being back in San Antonio was awkward. No one knew exactly what to say. The war was not a subject I wanted to discuss. It would have been better if I had discussed it rather than shutting down my feelings, but I couldn't discuss it with my family or anyone who hadn't been involved.

Because I had lost 20 pounds (I was almost six feet tall and now at 148 pounds) and because I had circles under my eyes from the celebration on the train and lack of sleep, my mother concluded that it had been a rough war. The first morning after my return my mother served scrambled eggs for breakfast. They looked great, but I couldn't eat them, recalling the green eggs of France. That upset her. I was sorry, but I would have choked had I tried. It took years before I could eat a scrambled egg. I still can't eat a Brussels sprout, a staple in the U.K.

There was a girl next door whom I had dated a few times

before I left Texas and then corresponded with while in Europe. Typically we read a lot between the lines. It was a buildup to a letdown. We thought a romance might materialize on my return, but we quickly realized there was no spark between us.

To renew contacts, I called several of the friends I had known before the war only to learn that none had made it back. The void in conversation after I heard the news from the family member was awkward and embarrassing. My favorite cousin and my best friend in high school had been killed, as had others. Thus I quit calling anyone I knew before the war. I decided to wait until I ran across them, or discovered what happened.

It was a new era. With thirty days leave I decided to have a good time before reporting to Washington, D.C., my next assignment. I had known Bucky McComas since we were fifteen and he was okay. His mother introduced me to her niece, Charlotte (Bucky's cousin). We dated while I was in San Antonio, and for a while thereafter. She had many friends in the area and introduced me to them. We attended parties, danced at the Fort Sam Houston Officers' Club on Saturday nights, and danced at some of the popular "juke joints" around San Antonio. At one of these night clubs a guy nearby leaned on the table and lit a cigarette while the National Anthem was being played! Infuriated, I was ready to let him know what I thought — that his actions were despicable. The rest of the people at the table restrained me. After the sacrifices that were made to defend the country I found his behavior unacceptable.

Being back in the States and having freedom of action without facing danger was a welcome change. Dancing and parties were enjoyable, but I wasn't comfortable having a good time. It didn't seem fair that I had returned unscathed and so many others hadn't.

I had the feeling that there wasn't a great deal of understanding in America of the war in Europe. Probably it wasn't possible to understand without being there or participating. Those who were living here couldn't imagine what those living in Europe, or the military forces, had experienced. My feelings toward those who hadn't been involved were not too charitable, especially those who complained about rationing of gasoline and butter. My adjustment from war to peace was too rapid, there was no period of deceleration, no discussion of what had occurred, no counseling. Fortunately I didn't have nightmares or psychological problems. I had it easy compared with the Army. It was just difficult to go from a war situation to one where it seemed that nothing had happened. But, as I've said, at the time I didn't want to discuss the war. I swept everything under the rug.

A good friend of Bucky's whom I had known, though not well, lost his right arm in combat. He felt his life had been ruined, drank entirely too much and smoked incessantly. A year or two later he was killed in an automobile accident while DUI. No one seemed able to reach him, to convince him that he had a life remaining. He was looking at what he had lost rather than appreciating the fact that he had survived, when many had not. But I can't say that I would have handled his situation any better than he did.

Herb Stucke was a good friend at Alamo Heights High School, who was voted the most popular guy in our senior class. He was killed during the war. Bob Mays was a super guy whom I knew in the National Guard and at Camp Bowie. Bob had a station wagon that he drove to San Antonio every weekend that he could and I used to ride with him, along with others, rather than drive my car. We would pay him a small amount to cover expenses. Bob asked me to drive the wagon one weekend when he couldn't get a pass and he had previously committed to drive passengers. I thought the wagon was unstable and didn't drive it again. Someone told me that Bob had been killed while driving the wagon.

The 36th Division, which I had belonged to at the beginning of my military career, played a key role in the invasion of Italy, landing at Anzio Beach, participating in one of the bloodiest battles of the war and suffering major losses. This fact makes me resent press criticism of those who joined the National Guard, making it appear that they were merely trying to avoid the draft. Many of the Guard units were mobilized and fought valiantly, upholding their history of valor. The men who joined the Guard preferred to join and serve in a unit with friends and neighbors. After the war I didn't try to locate any of the members of Company A. I was afraid to.

Reflections

As pilots in time of war, with a common goal, a common enemy, facing a common danger and at times dependent on each other for our lives, we formed a bond. When not flying combat, we didn't have a lot to do other than play cards, talk, or drink or perhaps all three at once. We lived together, ate together; certainly we had time to talk and time to get into serious discussions. It was possible for us to get to know each other at a deeper level than one would under ordinary circumstances. That made the loss more difficult to handle when pilots or crew members were killed.

Some of my close friends were in the 496th Squadron and a few were in other squadrons. It depended in part on scheduling and time off. What enabled any of us to survive is still a question. The saying, "The good die young," was definitely true in this situation. The pilots I knew were exceptional young men, and it seemed that many of the best were getting killed.

Johnny Eckert was the son of a major general, and a U.S. Military Academy graduate, who had honor and integrity, intelligence, ambition. He was great-looking, a super guy. We spent hours in discussion of deep subjects. This valued friend was lost in a midair collision.

Bill Geary was the type of guy whom everyone liked, always full of energy, always smiling, apparently having a great time despite the circumstances. It made me feel better just to be around him. He was killed in a crash on takeoff.

There were many others who were killed or wounded. It was a tragic waste. We were defending our country and our way of life after being attacked, but I had to question whether the war could have been avoided. The U.S. forces were totally inadequate when the war began. Had we maintained a strong military presence and an intelligence organization, would we not have deterred the buildup of German and Japanese military forces? Could we have stopped them? "The seeds of World War II were planted by the allies when they failed to stop German rearmament," said John Dos Passos. The attack on Pearl Harbor should not have happened, nor should it have been possible for the Japanese to destroy much of the Pacific fleet in the harbor. We paid a high price for being unprepared to defend our country.

Yet after World War II we destroyed our military aircraft and equipment, including all but a few B-26 Marauders. We again allowed our military forces to be depleted. The cold war, Korea and Vietnam followed and later the war with Iraq. Prior to each military operation there were diplomatic blunders that led us into the situation, a failure to understand what was occurring, or an incorrect assessment of what we were getting involved in and how to conduct the war. Of course none of these situations were called "war." The exception was the Gulf War where the requisite forces were marshalled, the goal was established and the field commander was allowed to make decisions on the use of his forces.

I'm not bitter, and I remain a patriot; it is my country, right or wrong. But I'd like to see us learn from our experience and stop wasting the lives of our best.

In take off position

On way to target

CHAPTER ELEVEN

WASHINGTON, D.C.

Assignment Pentagon

My assignment upon return from Europe was Headquarters, Army Air Forces, Washington, D.C., at the Pentagon, located in Northern Virginia. Although I was selected for assignment to the Operational Plans Division, the staff was cut and I was assigned to the Directorate of Intelligence, Intelligence Requirements Division, Collection Branch, as an Intelligence Staff Officer. The Collection Branch was responsible for obtaining intelligence information required by the Air Staff, for disseminating intelligence and for maintaining intelligence files. Much of the information was "Secret" or "Top Secret" and had to be controlled.

Millard Lewis, the brigadier general who headed the division, was a pioneer "who had lived through an entire decade of Air Corps efforts to obtain recognition for the combat plane as a primary instrument of warfare." He had flown some of the early bomber aircraft, the B-7, B-10 and B-18. He first flew the B-26 Marauder in 1941, recognizing both its potential and its characteristics, and was very involved with the B-26 in training and in combat. That was a plus as far as I was concerned, but it didn't really matter because as a captain, I rarely saw General Lewis and don't believe I talked to him more than once. As a captain I was too far down the line.

Major General Samuel Andersen also was a B-26 pioneer who headed the 9th Bomber Command, later the 9th Bombardment Division, composed of three wings and eleven bomb groups, a major part of the 9th Air Force. From November 1944 until May 1945 I had worked in 9th Bombardment Division Headquarters in operations. General Andersen was assigned to the Pentagon, and I did see him to seek his help regarding my career (more about that later.)

The chief of the collection branch to which I was assigned

was a major and a pilot. He and I were not in sync. The fact that we did not hit it off was definitely not to my advantage. Pilots had to fly a minimum number of hours a year to maintain qualification as a pilot and a minimum number of hours each month to qualify for flight pay. Flying the required hours was a problem for pilots assigned to desk jobs. Pilots assigned to the Pentagon flew out of Bolling Field in Washington, which was conveniently adjacent to the Naval Air Station and across the river from National Airport, now Reagan National. Any opportunity to fly was eagerly accepted because it was difficult to get away from the job and difficult to get a plane.

Depending on availability, a pilot on request could get a plane assigned for a cross-country training flight, and could ask another pilot to fly with him or have a copilot assigned. The major asked me to fly to Chicago with him one weekend. As pilot and aircraft commander it was a usual courtesy to ensure that the crew had accommodations and were taken care of, and it was customary to hang out with the other pilot. As soon as we landed, however, he announced the time we were to be present on the flight line the next day and promptly departed. We didn't see him again until it was time for takeoff. The weekend turned out to be both dull and expensive. His attitude annoyed me, and I'm sure I let my feelings show.

The work that we did in the Collection Branch was of great importance and very interesting to me. During my tenure in Collection, as an additional duty, I was assigned to be the Air Force representative to the Military Intelligence Services Reading Panel. As the Air Force representative, I selected intelligence reports deemed of interest to the Air Force from those distributed by other agencies and circulated through the panel. The time that could be devoted to an individual document was limited by the volume of reports. It was necessary to scan each quickly and to decide whether to request a copy of the document.

By chance, while on the Reading Panel I learned from a comment overheard that certain documents containing intelligence of utmost interest to the Air Force were being withheld by the Army. Of course I relayed this fact to my division chief and it was forwarded all the way up to Air Force chief of staff level, over to the counterpart Army level and back down to Army G-2, Intelligence Division. A major explosion resulted in the Pentagon, but a serious problem was brought to light and was resolved.

When I returned to the Reading Panel, the director, Colonel Charles Ralph Newton, directed me into his office and proceeded to call me every name he could think of. When he was through, he extended his hand and said, "Now that that's over, we can be friends." When he left Army Intelligence sometime later to work with the CIA, Colonel Newton asked me to come with him, which I appreciated, and though it might have been a wise choice to go with a new agency, at the time I was interested in an Air Force career.

The Army Air Force became a separate service in October 1947. It became the United States Air Force, or USAF. The Air Service had begun in 1918 as a part of the Signal Corps under the U.S. Army. Interestingly, my father had been assigned to the Air Service for a short time. The development of air power continued with pilots carrying the mail and engaging in experimental flying and air racing. General William Mitchell was one of the air pioneers who forecast the possibility of sinking ships and arranged a demonstration bombing of an obsolete ship. The results of the bombing did not make the Navy wildly enthusiastic. The B-25 Mitchell, twin-engine bomber and Mitchell Field were named for him.

Efforts to prove the value of air power continued and the value of achieving air supremacy and of the use of tactical and strategic bombardment was shown during World War II. Prior to WWII the development of air power was limited. It became more intense just before the U.S. entry into the war. Aircraft were being produced in large quantity on production lines. Training was enhanced, and strategy and tactics were being developed. Hitler had demonstrated the efficacy of air power in his attack on the countries of Poland and Czechoslovakia in Eastern Europe.

Pilots did not like the control of air operations by the Army, believing that the Army did not understand the proper use of air power, and the air pioneers fought for years for a separate service. Their efforts culminated in 1947 in the establishment of the USAF, and the placement of the three services, Army, Navy and Air, on a coequal basis.

Friction existed between the services. The Army and Navy each set up their own air arm in support of their service and there was disagreement over the roles of the air arm of the Army and of the Navy and the USAF. In an effort to resolve conflict, the Department of Defense, DOD, was established with a civilian secretary, a joint staff with a chairman of the joint chiefs of staff, and a chief of staff for each of the three services. This system has remained in effect since 1947, with defined roles for the Army, Navy and Air Force.

Application for the Regular Air Force

After World War II the Army opened applications for qualified active duty officers to apply for a regular commission. The competition was intense. After submitting my application, I continued to study current affairs, world affairs and military strategy to prepare for the interview with the selection board. Arriving fifteen minutes early for the interview, I expected to have time to get psyched for this important meeting, but as soon as I walked into the waiting room, my name was called, which I hadn't anticipated. This shook me because I had counted on the time to compose my thoughts. The board was a group of stern looking senior Army officers. I was nervous and did not handle the questioning well, although I knew the answers. My name was not on the selection list.

There was to be another selection opportunity so I went to see General Anderson to seek his advice and possible assistance. He learned that the major had not given me an outstanding effectiveness report and that a drop in effectiveness was not looked upon favorably by the board. Actually they were looking for any reason to eliminate an applicant because of the competition. The general said that I should have come to see him before the previous selection, and he offered to endorse my application for this round.

Because I had combat flying experience as well as staff experience at the Bombardment Division and Air Force Headquarters level, I believed I was a good applicant. This time I went before a board composed of Air Force officers. I was relaxed, and the board interview went very well; in fact it was most enjoyable. I was selected by the board and received a commission in the regular service of the USAF as a first lieutenant. At the same time I was a captain on active duty and a major in the Air Force reserve! Confusing.

My selection was important to me as it represented the achievement of an important goal, even though it was an Air Force career I chose, rather than the original Army career. As a regular Air Force officer I could stay on active duty with the Air Force until completion of 28 years of service, or until age 55 if I were a general officer. Being a career officer gave certain status.

Within the Air Force there was a situation at the time referred to as "the hump." Most of the officers brought into the regular service after the war were in the same age group, and the majority of them were in the grade of first lieutenant or captain. Competition for promotion was intense.

As a captain I had been selected to attend the Army Command and General Staff School at Fort Leavenworth, Kansas. Being selected for this school as a captain was a coup and completion of the course was very advantageous to a career in the military service. Unfortunately, the major decided he could not let me go at the time, but would let me attend a later course. He was transferred, however, and my experience and my presence were needed in the Collection Branch, thus I was not allowed to attend the course, which was detrimental to my career. Although I later was selected to attend the Air Command and Staff School at Maxwell Air Force Base, the potential career impact was not the same as it would have been earlier.

Accommodations

In Washington, D.C., in 1945 there was a shortage of housing. My sister, Dotty, and her husband, Frank, had a Tudor style house in North Arlington, Virginia, on North Greenbrier, and they invited me to live with them. We hadn't seen each other for some years, and I thought it would be enjoyable so I accepted. Because I paid a minimal rent my occupancy of the extra bedroom was helpful to both parties. Washington was expensive, and Air Force pay scales were not lavish.

Dotty and Frank had two charming young children, Pamela and Frank, Jr., known as Pam and Butch, and being with them was fun most of the time. My work at the Pentagon, flying and other activities kept me from spending much time at home. I was determined to like Washington and to make my stay there worthwhile. The girl next door, Emily Bowen, was a friend of Dotty's who was interested, as I was, in French lessons and in dancing lessons at Arthur Murray's, so we decided to take them together, which was fun. Emily was delightful and we dated for a while and had much in common, but there was no emotional tie other than friendship.

Frank was a colonel in the Air Force at the Pentagon who had served in Italy during the war. He was a pilot and had been a squadron commander at Brooks Field in San Antonio before the war. During a period of a few months, six of the pilots in his squadron were killed in plane crashes. As the wife of the squadron commander, Dotty had to call on the widows to console and assist them. It was unnerving for her. She became fearful and pleaded with Frank to stop flying. He ultimately acceded to her desires and requested suspension from flight status, which hurt his career. Ironically he was injured in a jeep accident in Italy during the war. Although he recovered, the neck injury he sustained has continued to plague him.

It was convenient for me to ride to and from the Pentagon with Frank as I didn't have a car. He strongly disliked being assigned to the Pentagon, however, and requested a transfer. They sold the house and left Washington. I thought of buying the house but it was over my head financially. Also it was not the right time, as my future was uncertain. I did not need a house, but it would have been a great investment. While they were showing the house, a nonrated lieutenant colonel came in to see it. He told me how rough it had been during the war. He had to commute between Washington and Baltimore, and there was gas rationing. I agreed that it must have been rough.

After a search I found a furnished room in D.C. but didn't

stay there long. The landlady was offensive and made things unpleasant. She watched me unpack "to see what I was bringing in," would go through my room when I was at work and did not allow visitors. Larry Turk, a pilot and friend, and I rented two rooms in a town house near George Washington University, which was convenient because I had started taking night classes. Larry married Carla, a lovely girl, and moved out. I moved to an apartment, thanks to a friend, Johnny Catlin.

Catlin and Scott

Johnny Catlin, an Air Force major, and a graduate of the U.S. Military Academy, class of January 1943, introduced me to a classmate, E.D. Scott, who had sublet an apartment on Pennsylvania Avenue near the White House. Johnny had flown a combat tour with the 344th Bomb Group, as I had, and also was assigned to the Pentagon. I didn't know him well in Europe because he was in a different squadron, but we became good friends while at the Pentagon and had lunch together frequently. Johnny would call and say, "Are you hungry?" He didn't need to identify himself; I knew the voice. He was married to a former Miss Florida and they were a striking couple. Audrey often invited me to dinner and it was a treat to be with them — they were both terrific people.

Scott was also a captain and a pilot. His father was a retired general who was married to a wealthy woman, Scott's stepmother, and lived in Palm Beach. One weekend Scott and I flew to Palm Beach for a visit and General and Mrs. Scott took us to lunch at an exclusive club. They were charming and hospitable people.

Before Scott and I were able to move into the apartment, he was killed in a plane crash on landing at the airfield at Marietta, Georgia. At his funeral I went up to speak to Mrs.

Scott not knowing how or what to communicate. She read my thoughts, preempted me and said, "There really isn't anything one can say, is there?" I had believed that after the war I wouldn't be continually confronted with the death of my friends, but I was wrong.

It was awkward trying to determine what to do about the apartment. In a way I didn't want to move in and there was the problem of a roommate. Johnny suggested that I assume the sublease and introduced me to another classmate, Joe Hamilton, who was looking for someone to share an apartment. When Hamilton was transferred, Major Wendell Bevan, a pilot, and the son of an Army colonel, moved in.

The apartment was leased to an artist, who had decorated it very well. There were two large rooms furnished as studios, each with a fireplace, a small kitchen and a balcony overlooking Pennsylvania Avenue. It was four blocks from the White House, a very convenient location for all our friends to drop by for a drink when they were in the city. We had a standing party every Saturday night. Bev was always the life of the party. We had an occasional stranger come up from the street to join the party; Bev and I both would think that the other had invited him until we compared notes after the party.

Johnny Catlin agreed to fly an Army friend up to West Point for a visit over a weekend. He was flying an AT-6, a single-engine, two-seater training plane. It could be tricky for a twin-engine pilot not familiar with it. On my first flight out of Bolling I almost put one into the Potomac on landing. I don't think Johnny had flown the AT-6 much, but I don't believe that was the problem. On the return flight from Stewart Field to Washington, Johnny's plane disappeared shortly after takeoff. There was no radio contact. The search for the plane continued for seven days. Initially everyone was hoping they would be found still alive.

Audrey was handling the situation very well in the beginning, and I admired her for it, but after a few days hope began to fade. Audrey asked me to drive Johnny's convertible back from Bolling where he had parked it before takeoff on that fateful flight. When I pulled into their driveway, went into the house and handed Audrey the keys to the car, she broke down. It was then that she had the realization that Johnny wouldn't be returning. The plane was found after a week's search; it had flown into a mountain in a heavily forested area, which made it difficult to locate.

Audrey asked me to be an honorary pallbearer. The funeral at Fort Myer, Virginia, provided full military honors, with the Army band, horses drawing the caisson bearing the casket, an overflight of planes with one missing from the formation, and at the burial site the requisite volleys of rifle fire and the playing of taps. The honorary pallbearers were required to march behind the caisson from the chapel to the grave site. As I marched, looking at the casket and thinking of the great friend I had lost and of Audrey, and of others, tears ran slowly down my face.

Johnny's death seemed so ironic, after he had completed a combat tour in a B-26 Marauder, to be killed on a routine flight. I didn't understand why. Johnny was such a super guy and he and Audrey were supremely happy. I began to feel that as a friend I was a jinx and made the decision not to have any more pilots as close friends.

Moving On

When the artist who sublet the apartment returned to Washington, Bev and I had to move. We took an apartment on Riggs Road, in Northeast Washington. It was a great apartment but not conveniently located. Bev left to get married. I moved into a bachelor house in North Arlington. It was a large house on three acres of ground, with a ballroom on the third floor. Seven officers lived there and we had a live-in maid. It was a great place to live and a great place for parties. I had a Halloween costume party in the ballroom that became the party of the year, with a band and dancing. There were six auto accidents after the party, and one of the house members broke his leg. He was a pilot who had saved all his money, very tight, and he was killed about a year later in a Jeep accident. I decided not to save money but to enjoy spending it.

Friends

In Washington I developed three sets of friends: native Washingtonians, known as cave dwellers; military officers; and political types. I was having a wonderful time. An Army friend, Bob Beightler, who was a White House Aide, had my name placed on the Washington social list, and I was invited to quite a few debutante balls and various parties around Washington. One party was at the Sulgrave Club, where I met and danced with Margaret Truman, who was quite attractive. Of course I wrote home to say that I had danced with the President's daughter. In a magazine article that I read subsequently, Margaret stated that she wondered if the young men danced with her because they wanted to, or so they could write home about it. I'm sure it was because they wanted to.

Meeting the President

A large party was given at the home of one of the White House aides in Georgetown. Arriving late I had to park a couple of blocks away. The street was cordoned off and a number of black limousines were parked in front of the house. Secret Service men were much in evidence. The first floor of the house was crowded so I went down the steps to the basement recreation room. At the foot of the stairs I saw President and Mrs. Truman talking to several people. As I reached the bottom of the stairs, the President turned toward me, stuck out his hand and said, "Truman." I said, "Yes, I know, Mr. President." He introduced me to Mrs. Truman and I stayed and talked for a few minutes. The President said that his fondest recollections were of the times he spent with military personnel. He had been a captain of artillery in World War I, and had the rank of colonel in the Reserve. During the conversation he stated that someone had asked him what he wanted on his tombstone and he replied, "Here lies Harry Truman, he did his damnedest." He was very easy to talk to. I believe he was a courageous President, who made important decisions, such as dropping the atom bomb, instituting the Marshall Plan to restore Western Europe after WWII, and firing General MacArthur during the Korean War. Although I had disagreed at the time with Truman's firing of a general whom I admired, after reading about what occurred, I don't believe he could have done otherwise. An important principle of civilian control over the military forces was involved. I heard MacArthur speak at the Union League in Philadelphia not long before he died, and he was impressive even then.

Unlikely Events

Tragedy struck once more very close to me, against three young ladies whom I met in Washington. The three were very attractive and prominent socially. Jean Mears, who was married to my then-boss, Lieutenant Colonel Frank Mears, introduced me to Edwina Pou Wadden, a cave dweller, as native Washingtonians were often referred to. Her family were friends of several presidents including Roosevelt. The Waddens lived in a huge apartment opposite the Shoreham Hotel. The building has since been destroyed and replaced with something of lesser quality. Through Eddie Pou, whom I dated until she left for Paris, I met Lelia Noyes, a beauty whose family published the *Evening Star*, a leading

Washington newspaper at, the time, but no longer in existence. Another friend was Margaret Thors, the daughter of the Icelandic Minister to Washington.

I introduced Lelia to Dave Thompson, a close friend, and Margaret to Tom Hallahan. Dave and Tom were house-mates of mine at the time. Both introductions resulted in romances that were heavy for a while, but didn't last.

Strangely and sadly, all three of these lovely young women who were close friends died in their twenties. Eddie Pou went to work for the U.N. Ambassador in Paris and died there of a cerebral hemorrhage at age 25. Lelia gave up on Dave as he was commitment-shy, having been married before, and she married a Marine major, who was transferred to London. Lelia died while in London; I don't know the cause. Margaret allegedly committed suicide, although I'll never know why. She was beautiful, intelligent, charming and wealthy. A tragic waste!

Animal House

The big house that we lived in was sold so another move ensued, to a house off Ridge Road in Arlington. There was a conflict within the house so I leased a house in Lyon Village, Arlington, with five bedrooms and four baths, and got four other officers to move in. Annie Mae quit her job on Ridge Road and came to work for me. (I didn't influence the decision. She had left her job before contacting me.) Prior to our moving in, the neighbor next door tried unsuccessfully to get an injunction to prevent it, considering a group of bachelors undesirable for the neighborhood. When we had our first party she called the police although the party wasn't noisy. She objected to the cars parked on the street. After a while she accepted the fact that we were going to stay. The house worked out well after a bad start, but the activity level wasn't conducive to studying. There were too many diversions.

Completing an Education

The Air Force selected a small group of officers to return to school to obtain a degree. In order to qualify for admission to the education program it was necessary to be able to complete the requirements for a bachelor's degree in two years. Selections were made competitively. Hoping to attend the University of Texas, I applied, but the Air Force sent me to The George Washington University in Washington, D.C. That was disappointing, but I was fortunate to be selected, as I believed a degree was important to advancement in the service.

Having had my activities restricted while training for war and fighting the war, I was geared to make up for lost time. Although I didn't look my age, I felt I was too old to join a fraternity. However, after receiving bids from SAE, Sigma Chi and Pi Kappa Alpha, and as many of their members were veterans, I accepted the bid from PiKA, where my friend from San Antonio, Brooke Jones, was a member. The Pikes had a beautiful house on Massachusetts Avenue and a good group of members, including most of the athletes at GWU, and there were many parties in the basement party room, which had a large bar.

It was difficult to return to being a full-time student, although easier than working and going to night school, as I had done for two years. GWU gave no credit for service schools and only two hours for the business school in San Antonio. I had to complete three years of work in two, which meant attending all year round for two years. There was no problem grasping the information, but some of the classes were boring and it was hard for me to study when there were many more interesting things to do. I did get a BA degree in business administration with a reasonable grade average.

Love at First Sight

As the lessee of the house I was living in, I also had the responsibility for maintaining it. None of the other house residents were at all helpful. One fine day as I was cutting the grass, a gorgeous redhead driving by in a black Cadillac was forced to stop because of a truck blocking the road. We coolly appraised each other. The thought crossed my mind, "Wouldn't it be strange if she were the girl that I married?" That evening and for a week or more thereafter I cased the neighborhood looking for the car to find out where she lived. Having had an unsuccessful search, I asked Quinn Elson, a teenager who lived next door, whether he knew anything about her. He told me that her name was Joanne Turney, that she lived in the next block, was single and attended GWU.

After checking out the campus, I found her in the bookstore one day and introduced myself, asking if she lived in Lyon Village and if she drove a black Cadillac. She still swears that it was the other way around, and that I first asked about the Cadillac. When I started calling to take her out she was always "busy." Finally I asked when she would not be busy and got a date. One of the PiKAs was surprised that she dated me because she was supposedly pinned to another member of the fraternity. Nevertheless, we continued to date, and she broke up with Frank.

Joanne had been a leading candidate for "Dream Girl" of PiKA and was runner up for Homecoming Queen at GWU. She knew most of the brothers, but I hadn't seen her at the PiKA house. After we started dating, we often attended parties at the fraternity house and at Bolling Field Officers' Club, and went dancing at the Shoreham. By that time I had realized my dream of owning a Buick convertible, which enhanced my status with Joanne as well as at the fraternity house. The Buick, however, was giving me problems and about to give up the ghost after a couple of years, so I traded it for a Packard convertible, a rather flashy car, turquoise-blue with a tan top and red leather upholstery. It was the only Packard convertible available at the time, and I had to trade fast. It worked out because the car had class, a long hood with a Cormorant as the hood ornament. The GWU school colors were buff and blue. So Jo Spaulding, who dated a fraternity brother, and who had a buff Cadillac convertible, and I, in the turquoise-blue Packard, were selected to lead the school parades.

Joanne Turney was a Delta Gamma at GWU, majoring in sociology with a minor in psychology and philosophy. These were not my favorite subjects. We had a shared interest in dancing and social activities, having a good time. Now we enjoy music, art and travel. Born in San Diego, which was her mother's home town, Joanne had spent most of her life on either the west or east coast, in San Diego or in Washington, D.C., depending on her Naval officer father's station. I was very fond of her parents and they approved of me. Joanne and I enjoyed being together and we fell in love. After we had dated for about ten months, I proposed. We became engaged just before the Korean conflict began, and we set the wedding date three months hence, for September 29, 1950, not knowing whether I would go to Korea. We were in that state of bliss known as love and Joanne's parents approved of our engagement. More important Annie Mae, the housekeeper, approved and she okayed the ring before I presented it to Joanne.

Joanne's father was then a Navy captain; thus the wedding took place at the Naval Communications Chapel on Nebraska Avenue in Washington, and the reception was at the Bethesda Medical Center Officers Club. What started out to be a small wedding grew to encompass about 300 guests.. There were Army, Navy and Marine ushers. PiKAs and Delta

Gammas as well as all our friends and the Turneys' friends and relatives attended. My sister was the only one from my family who could attend. It was a wonderful party and we were almost the last to leave, because we were departing Washington and felt that we wouldn't see many of the guests again.

Bermuda and St. Louis, Louis

Before the wedding I had to complete the degree requirements, finish my courses, graduate, turn over the house and prepare for transfer to St. Louis, Missouri, where the Air Force had assigned me. As I was being awarded a degree in business administration, I was assigned to the Air Force Audit organization, known as the Auditor General. Because there were few officers in the Air Force with accounting, audit and administrative qualifications, I was awarded a Military Occupational Specialty (MOS) in a Limited Resource category, Accountant-Auditor Staff, which virtually prevented transfer out of the Auditor General organization.

For our wedding trip we flew to Bermuda and stayed at Cambridge Beaches in Somerset, located at the west end of the island. The hotel had individual cottages, each with a private beach, and a main dining room in a central building. Cambridge Beaches was a good choice as it had an air of enchantment. The island was beautiful. We met another couple, the Owsley Hills from Houston, and we became great friends but never encountered them again. The four of us went deep-sea fishing and a squall came up. The skipper cut the engines, to ride out the storm, which I understand is the wrong thing to do. Coral reefs were all around us and I could visualize the headlines: "Honeymoon couples drowned off the coast of Bermuda." We survived, but for breakfast I'd had fried eggs, and it was the closest I've ever come to being seasick.

At that time few automobiles were allowed in Bermuda, but there were taxis that took us on a tour of the island. Shopping was interesting, as the British governed the island and British products were predominant. We used checks received as wedding gifts to purchase crystal water and champagne glasses and a large white damask tablecloth.

Joanne's engagement picture

The Packard

The Buick

170

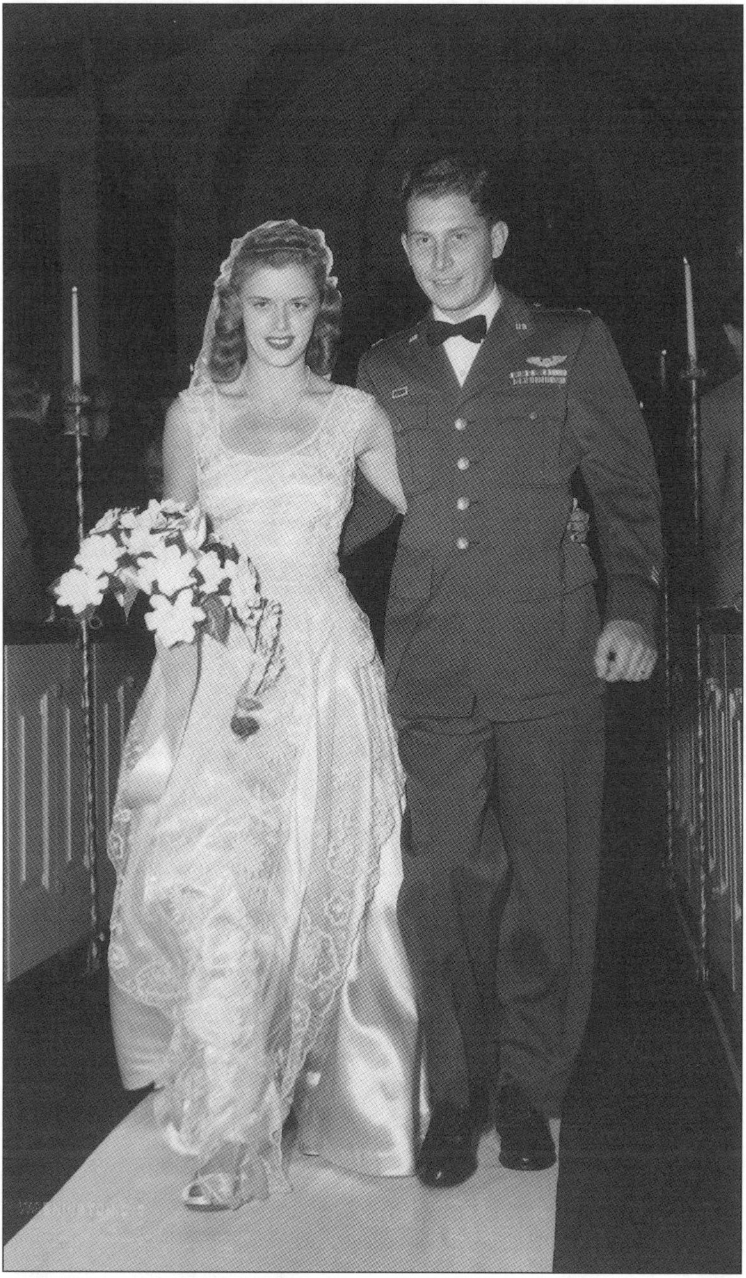

CHAPTER TWELVE

LIFE IN THE AUDITOR GENERAL ORGANIZATION

St. Louis

On return from Bermuda we drove all the way from Washington to San Antonio in the Packard with the top down, made possible by the Indian summer weather. En route to Texas we visited Maxwell AFB Montgomery, Alabama, where Dotty and Frank were stationed, and the New Orleans French Quarter. In San Antonio we visited my parents, who gave a big party for us to introduce Joanne to family and friends there. From San Antonio it was on to St. Louis, Missouri where the Auditor General regional office was located.

We found an apartment in St. Louis Hills in a four-unit building. With the money that was left after the ring purchase and the trip to Bermuda, we purchased furniture and Joanne made the draperies. The occupants of the other two rented apartments were Warren and Ella Rose, who were young, married a year or two, and expecting, and Gene and Electra Dobbs, who were older, in their forties. The six of us became fast friends. We got together for drinks almost every evening and had a really good time.

Shortly after arrival in St. Louis, Joanne and I both developed a wicked viral bronchitis and became really ill. We were saved by the treatment of my friend, Warren Lonergan, an internist, who lived in St. Louis, who had been a flight surgeon in the 344th Bomb Group in Europe. Electra's kindness in cooking meals for us and leaving them at the door sustained us. I didn't like the cold weather in St. Louis, the frozen door locks in the morning, and driving in snow and ice. The office didn't do much for me, either. After three months in St. Louis, just as we were settled, I was sent to Albany, Georgia, as acting resident auditor. It seemed likely that we would not return to St. Louis, so we placed the furniture in storage, gave up the lease on the apartment, and drove to Albany, where we rented a small furnished apartment. We loved Albany, but we were there just a short time before being assigned to Atlanta.

Atlanta

In Atlanta, the new Southeastern District Headquarters, was being formed, one of six districts in the revised Auditor General organization. My job was chief, technical division, with responsibility for audit supervision of 24 offices in a five-state area. It required periodic visits to each office, usually for a week at a time. Joanne accompanied me on most of the trips, and we had a good time driving the Packard, staying in different places, and meeting people. The per diem allowance was $5 a day and I believe mileage allowance was five cents a mile, so we lodged in bed-and-breakfast places or inexpensive motels and lived frugally.

My follow-on assignment was as chief, administrative division, which was a spot for a colonel. As I was then a major there was a lot of opportunity coupled with responsibility. The district chief, Colonel George Hinckley, liked and respected me and vice versa and I enjoyed Atlanta and my job.

We bought a house that was under construction, on Moores Mill Road near Paces Ferry Road, using the GI bill with $750 down. It was an inexpensive house in an expensive neighborhood. While waiting for its completion we lived in a furnished rental house. Walking in the neighborhood, we met Ricky Carter who lived nearby in a house with a swimming pool. We hit it off immediately and became close friends. Ricky was good-looking with dark hair and eyes and liked having a good time. He had been married and divorced, and dated a succession of women. A former Air Force pilot, he had his own small plane, which he rarely flew and did not properly maintain.

After one flight in his plane, a bird's nest was discovered in the cowling and the plane with bird's nest and eggs was pictured on the front page of an Atlanta paper. Ricky thereafter bragged that he could land a plane without breaking an egg.

It seemed that our new house would never be finished and finally I insisted on a guarantee in writing that we could move in by September 1, 1951. We moved in but there were no utilities connected. Utilities had not been specified in the agreement! We decided to move in anyway, and the contractor ran a wire in for electricity. On the Saturday the van with our furniture was to arrive, we waited all day in vain, sitting on the bare floor. Early on Sunday morning the van arrived, but the driver couldn't get any help to unload. We had the choice of unloading the van ourselves or waiting until the driver offloaded other shipments in another city and returned. I called Ricky, and he came right over to help unload. Ricky and I submitted invoices for our labor — and got paid. The money was used for a steak dinner.

One day I admired a shirt that Rick was wearing and he took it off and gave it to me. He literally gave me the shirt off his back.

After we moved into our new home, we had a housewarming to which we invited Colonel Hinckley, the district chief, and several others from the office. Ricky arrived late and loaded, careening into the driveway with tires screeching. He propped his date up against the wall and, while everyone was still in shock, bet the group that he could drink a glass of water while standing on his head. He did! Then he bet that he could touch the ceiling fixture in the party room with his foot, which he did, albeit a little too forcefully. (He replaced the fixture.) By that time the group was in the palm of his hand, and we had quite a party.

Fort Worth, Texas

About a year after we moved into our house, federal cutbacks forced the closing of two of the six districts. The Southeastern district was one of them; it was discouraging because our District was the most effective of the six. I tried to place all civil-service personnel who were not accepting transfers or who had not been offered transfers to Southwestern District in Fort Worth, which was absorbing Southeastern's responsibilities. The S.W. District was not giving our civilian personnel the rights due them, so I appealed to the Civil Service Commission in Washington. This action put me in the doghouse with the chief, S.W. District, and my name was mud in Fort Worth. But it was the right thing to do. We had to sell the house and move to Fort Worth to a rental apartment, moving in when the temperature was 106°F degrees and Joanne was expecting. It was a difficult time. Fortunately, I had been selected for the Air Command and Staff School at Maxwell AFB, Montgomery, Alabama and after about five months was able to leave Fort Worth, where I was persona non grata with the district chief.

Initially after leaving Atlanta we kept in touch with Ricky but then we didn't hear from him for quite a while. I contacted his partner, who told me that Ricky had been electrocuted while sanding the deck of his boat. Inadvertently he had touched the water with his foot. Jack had prophesied that Ricky would kill himself because he had no regard for electricity, and he was in the construction business. Jack's prophecy was unhappily right. Joanne and I regard Ricky as the most unforgettable character we've met.

Montgomery, Alabama

While we were in Montgomery, and I was attending the Air Command and Staff School at Maxwell Air Force Base, we lived in a house that had been converted into three apartments. Joanne was expecting our first child, previously having had a miscarriage in Atlanta, which had been upsetting for both of us. In Montgomery she was bitten by a neighbor's dog and couldn't take a tetanus shot. She started hemorrhaging and was confined to bed. She got past that but the situation was wearing. Meanwhile I was attending an important school and trying to do my best. At night while I was studying, there was a great deal of noise upstairs, so I lodged a complaint with the agent. One Sunday morning as we were going to church, an absolutely sensational-looking woman was getting into her car in front of the house. She looked up at me while batting her eyelashes and said, "I understand you've been bothered by the noise from my apartment." I responded, "Oh no, it hasn't bothered me a bit." Joanne has not yet let me forget this incident.

Our daughter, Christine, was born in Montgomery, when I was about halfway through school. We selected that name because she was born on Good Friday. On Easter Sunday I brought Chris a big yellow stuffed rabbit, about twice her size. The nurses derived some amusement from it. It was great having a baby, although the timing wasn't great. I had to complete the course and following completion we had to drive to Philadelphia, where I was to be stationed and find a place to live. Meanwhile, we were living out of suitcases and duffel bags.

Joanne's OB had insisted she remain in bed for two weeks after Chris was born. Joanne's mother came down to stay for those two weeks to take care of the baby, but she left about the time Joanne, weak from staying in bed, was allowed to get up. It was a tough time. Chris was on formula, on demand feeding, and she demanded feeding about every two hours. We were not getting any sleep. The school was difficult, and though I don't know how, I graduated. On leaving

Montgomery I was so tired that I had to stop the car and take a nap before I could proceed. Joanne was a real trouper, taking care of the baby and tolerating the situation without complaint.

Philadelphia

From Maxwell I was assigned to the Auditor General Headquarters in Philadelphia thanks to my friend Lieutenant Colonel Ed Beaty who was stationed there. I was grateful that I didn't have to return to Fort Worth. Colonel James Irwin, who was in charge of the office, asked me to take on the job of chief of personnel, which I accepted. There were 2,500 people in the organization: officers, airmen and civilians. This meant there were three sets of regulations and offices all over the world. The job was difficult and challenging but I liked it and got along well with Colonel Irwin, though not too well with my supervisor, a lieutenant colonel, or his assistant, a major. They were both Reserve officers who had tried and failed to get regular commissions and had been relieved from active duty. They received promotions in the reserve and were recalled to active duty in those grades, outranking me. I was resentful and didn't believe either was qualified for his job, though I liked them both personally.

Flying was out of McGuire AFB in New Jersey. In order to fly I had to request time off from the office, get a plane assigned and then drive to McGuire from our home in Wayne, Pennsylvania. It required getting up about four in the morning and making the two-hour drive to the airbase. Often when I arrived I found that the plane was out for maintenance or had not returned from cross-country, or the weather did not permit flying. So I would drive back to Philadelphia and go to work. It was frustrating and I got static from the non-rated officers who regarded the time spent flying as a day off.

We had found a house in Wayne, that we liked. Miraculously, while looking around the area we drove by the house of some friends, Chuck and Ruth Thornton. Chuck was stationed in Philadelphia with the auditor general. We had no idea where they lived and saw their name on a mailbox on Croton Road! We knocked on the door and they were as surprised as we were. They advised us that the model house in the subdivision was for sale, and we bought it. The house was on an acre of ground, built of stone and desert brick, with open beamed ceilings, a stone fireplace in the living room, four bedrooms and two baths, and a two-car carport. It was perfect and within our price range.

While we lived in Wayne our second child, Joanne Louise, named after her mother and grandmother but called Joni, was born at Valley Forge. We employed a nurse, Mrs. McGillicuddy, nicknamed Gilly, to take care of Joni for two weeks after she came home. Gilly put Joni on a schedule, and it worked out fine. We tried not to pay too much attention to the baby so as not to upset Chris. When Gilly left, Chris who was then two, said, "Gilly forgot to take her baby."

Joni was a very good baby, placid and happy. She hardly ever cried and would sit in her stroller or amuse herself in the playpen for hours. As Chris and Joni were just two years apart, they were able to play together while growing up and to enjoy it most of the time. Both children were well behaved and drew praise from observers for their behavior. The situation changed somewhat in their late teens. In the interim we enjoyed being with them and had enjoyable vacations at Rehoboth Beach, Delaware, and in Spain, on the Costa del Sol, or visiting their paternal grandparents in San Antonio.

We had good friends, the Gardners and the Thorntons, and enjoyed our life in Wayne, but the days were long. I had to catch the commuter train to Philadelphia at 7:00 A.M. and returned home about 7:00 P.M. If Joanne wanted the car, she had to drive me to the station and pick me up. Chuck Thornton and I would trade rides, so it wasn't too onerous, and Ruth and Joanne were able to get together. After a while we bought a second car. Life was good, but then the Auditor General Headquarters was transferred to Washington. It was after the fact when I heard about it. Personnel who had bought homes in the Philadelphia area were not considered for transfer, whereas we would gladly have sold the house and moved to D.C. if given the choice. Joanne's parents lived in Northern Virginia and the D.C. area was like hometown to both of us, as we had lived, gone to school and been married in D.C.

There seemed to be no future in Philly after the Headquarters was transferred. At one point I was scheduled to take over the audit office in Hawaii, but the civilian in charge decided not to leave. So I went to Air Force Personnel in Washington to ask about transfer out of the Auditor General. The only two choices possible with sufficient priority to get me out of the organization and the limited resource specialty were flying refueling aircraft or cargo planes in Korea or attaché duty. Naturally, I applied for attaché duty and was selected with assignment to Bangkok. We were quite pleased and advertised our house with the lead in the classified ad, "Sailing for Siam." That assignment fell through, and we were soon advertising "Packing for Pakistan." To no avail, I might add. The house was vacant for a year before we sold it at a loss. It did not have a basement, which was almost essential in the area.

CHAPTER THIRTEEN

ATTACHÉ DUTY - PAKISTAN

To Meet
Major Frank W. Bauers, Jr.
United States Assistant Air Attache-Designate
and Mrs. Bauers
Major and Mrs. Warren E. Reid
request the pleasure of the company of

at a reception
on Wednesday May 23rd
at 43/2/J Drigh Road

R.S.V.P.
Tel. 7341

7:30 9:30 p.m.

The Attaché Course

Prospective attachés were required to complete a six-month course at the Strategic Intelligence School in Washington before going on station. We drove to Washington and leased an apartment at Arlington Towers in Rosslyn, Virginia. Unfortunately, Joanne's father, Admiral Turney, had died of lung cancer, at age 56, just before we were to move. We decided to cancel the lease and stay with Joanne's mother while we were in Washington. Staying with her was helpful to all of us. I completed the course during this difficult time and prepared for assignment in Karachi. Previously, attachés to Pakistan were sent to language school to learn Urdu, but that was discontinued as the majority of Pakistanis, and certainly all those with whom we dealt, were fluent in English. Many had attended schools in England or the United States On occasion it would have been helpful to have the ability to speak Urdu but it wasn't necessary.

As an assistant air attaché, I was required to buy uniforms, epaulettes, dinner jackets, day and evening clothes for Madame, china and glassware for entertaining, and electrical appliances that had either been converted to 220 volts or were capable of operating with a transformer. I also had to pay to ship a car from the United States to Pakistan as it was essential to have one there. We shipped the previously owned black Cadillac sedan we had purchased in Philadelphia, and sold the Packard. We had to sell securities in order to meet all the expenditures.

We had to separate our furnishings, clothing, and personal belongings into three categories: those items for storage, those for shipment and those to accompany us on the flight. Actually there was a fourth category, for express shipment to Karachi. Again, it was a hectic period. Of course our winter coats and blankets, which we did not need, were sent to Karachi and our pillows went to storage, despite our efforts.

To London, Paris, Rome, Beirut and Karachi

We left Washington on Pan American Airways out of New York, departing for London, Paris, Rome, Beirut and Karachi. The children were one and three. We had twelve pieces of luggage, a folding baby bed and a stroller. It was necessary to take two taxis in London to transport the entourage and baggage. I had asked for delay en route, charged as leave of absence, so we could spend time in London, Paris and Rome.

For the flight from New York to London, we had arranged sleeping berths on the Boeing Stratocruiser, believing that this would allow us to sleep through the night and arrive in London well rested. After cocktails in the lounge and then dinner, we climbed into the berths about 11:00 P.M., having neglected to note the five-hour time change between New York and London. Shortly after we climbed into the berths, breakfast was announced and we had to prepare for landing in London at what was for us, three o'clock in the morning, eight o'clock London time.

In Paris we stayed with friends, Herb and Lois Engelbrecht. Herb had been in the 344th Bomb Group at the same time I was. Although he was in a different squadron, we were on the same pass schedules and had made numerous trips to London together. Herb was outgoing and always was in a good mood — great fun to be with. I had attended the wedding of Herb and Lois in New Jersey after the war. It was three days of nonstop eating and celebration, before, during and after the wedding. They took us around Paris and made our visit enjoyable.

We checked in at the Paris airport for the flight to Rome, but for reasons unknown the flight takeoff was delayed for five hours. Joni sat in her stroller for the entire time without making a sound. A man walked over to where we were sitting and said, "That is the best baby I have ever seen!" He introduced himself, and gave me his card, Curtis Johnson, IV (president of Johnson Wax Co.).

On arrival in Rome we went to the Hotel Bernini Bristol to check in. The clerk said that the reservation had been canceled because of the delay in arrival. He also said that no other rooms were available in Rome. My response was, "Then we'll just have to sleep in the lobby," and we sat down on a sofa. A short time later the desk clerk said, "We have a suite for you." Probably our diplomatic passports encouraged the desk to accommodate us, or perhaps they just didn't want us to clutter the lobby.

We arranged a bus sight-seeing tour of Rome, but it was difficult for us with the children and the stroller to negotiate the steps and to keep up with the group. We opted out of the tour and got a taxi to take us to the Coliseum, the Vatican and other places of interest. Rome is a wonderful city and we enjoyed our visit there.

Beirut, then known as the Paris of the East, was the last stop en route to Karachi. We didn't see much of Beirut that trip but did spend time there on other trips from Karachi to Europe and return. It was quite a city before all the destruction occasioned by bombings and military action.

As the plane was coming in for a landing in Karachi, I could look down and see the shacks of the homeless refugees, as well as donkey carts and camels, and I wondered what I had done to my family. Pakistan had been formed as a separate state out of India. The Muslims had fought for an independent state and separation from the Hindus. They achieved independence in 1947 with the partition of India into two countries: India, in the central portion, and a two-part state,

East and West Pakistan, on either side of India. Ultimately, East Pakistan, formerly Bengal, broke away to become Bangladesh, but it was long after we had left.

Karachi

Before leaving I accompanied Joanne to Nan Duskin's in Philadelphia to purchase a suit for the trip. It was a designer tweed suit with a brown velvet collar, and Joanne altered a hat to match with a brown velvet brim. It had been cold in Europe, so she was wearing the suit and mink stole when we arrived in Karachi. The temperature on the tarmac was about 120 degrees. The attaché, Colonel Clint True and Mrs. True (known as "Tinkie") and the attaché staff were there to greet us. While we were meeting and greeting, Joni's stroller collapsed, and she was sitting on the tarmac. Tinkie would break up later whenever she thought of Joanne in the suit, hat and mink stole in that heat and Joni practically sitting on the sizzling asphalt and not complaining.

Major Warren Reid was my predecessor as assistant air attaché. He and Althea had arranged for our stay at their home, 43 2 J Drigh Road, which was to be passed on to us along with all the servants upon their departure a week hence. They also had arranged a reception to introduce us to about 300 people the following night. We were exhausted from the trip and the stress. Joanne had laryngitis and couldn't talk, and both the children had broken out in huge welts from septic heat rash. However, the show must go on.

At the reception we were introduced to the attachés from other countries, Pakistan Air Force officers, government officials and Karachi society. The names all had different sounds from those we were accustomed to. Before the party I reviewed the guest list and pictures of some of the more important people so I would have a clue as to who they were:

I wanted to connect names and faces. After the party I looked at the pictures taken and asked Warren to identify the people I couldn't recall. All this helped but it was still a challenge. The guests were meeting one couple and we were meeting 300 people, so they were better able to remember us, but we did okay.

As attachés we were members of the Ambassador's staff with the responsibility for advising the ambassador on air matters; representing the USAF; liaison with the Pakistan Air Force; and overt collection of information. Shortly after our arrival, Warren drove me to the U.S. Embassy to show me around. He drove up to an old building with a used-car show room on the first floor and said, "This is the U.S. Embassy." I laughed, thinking it a joke, but it wasn't. Our offices were on the second floor and they were barely adequate, minimum standard, and totally lacking in prestige. We had, however, a good staff in the office and that was more important. A new embassy structure had been planned, to be built in Karachi, but instead it was built in Islamabad, the location of the new capitol established after our departure.

The air attaché, Colonel True, was a graduate of West Point where he had been a football star. During WWII he was awarded the Distinguished Service Cross, which ranks just below the Medal of Honor. He was impressive-looking but had a difficult personality. While he could be charming, he had an exalted ego, was quite sarcastic, and often vindictive, and was not terribly interested in working. For fourteen years he had been a colonel and should have been a general, but his attitude and acerbic tongue probably kept him from it. He blamed Tinkie, who had a drinking problem, for his not being promoted, and she blamed him for her drinking. On return to the United States they were divorced, but meanwhile they made our life in Karachi interesting. They were delightful most of the time. The attaché had a beach house, and we had a carte blanche invitation to use it. The Trues entertained a great deal at home and we were always invited to their parties. We enjoyed their company until Tinkie had had too much to drink, and then it was awkward and sometimes embarrassing.

As attachés, we were invited to at least one and often two or three parties every night. These were glittering affairs with officers in uniform and diplomats in black tie, and the ladies in beautiful gowns or saris with exquisite jewelry. Each country had a national day, or a king's, a queen's or a president's birthday to celebrate. There were parties for important visitors, parties for arriving and departing dignitaries, parties for national holidays, and military parties for promotions, arrivals and departures. Once a month there were attaché parties. There were informal parties. We enjoyed the parties, but said, "Never on Sundays," and limited our drinking. We usually ate dinner before going out and ate very little at the parties. There were three reasons for limiting our intake: It was difficult to get to the buffet table because people would crowd around it and stand there; it was awkward to hold a drink and eat standing up; flies were abundant and there were generally no screens, so the flies would swarm over the food.

The social life was important to our work. It was important to meet and get to know people and know what was going on. We also had to work a full schedule at the office, starting at 7:00 A.M. Theoretically we were to get off at 1:00 P.M., but we usually were not able to leave the office until much later. We had to meet all visiting U.S. officials and dignitaries arriving at the Mauripur airport, which was across town, and there were quite a few VIPs coming through.

We met Vice-President and Mrs. Nixon. We thought that the VP handled himself very well with questions about Kashmir, still in contention, and that Mrs. Nixon was exceedingly well groomed, charming and gracious. She knew exactly what to say to each person she met. We met senators, congressmen, ambassadors, kings and princes and four-star generals. Almost all of the important people were easy to meet and to talk to. A few of the generals' aides were the most difficult.

About three weeks after our arrival, we encountered a man from East Pakistan at the ambassador's, Fourth of July party. He was paying a lot of attention to Joanne, and it was beginning to annoy both her and me. I asked who he was and was told that he was H.S. Suhrwardy, likely to become the next prime minister of Pakistan. Shortly thereafter we received an invitation to his home for swimming, dinner and dancing. We declined. As predicted, he became prime minister. For a while we were ignored, but then we received an invitation from him. At another party beforehand we encountered him, and he said with an amused smile, "When I invited you to my party before, you didn't come. Now I'm prime minister and you have to come." An invitation from him was for us a command performance. We went. He had official parties as prime minister with hundreds of people attending, and private parties with 30 or 40 guests. We were invited to both types of events.

We had the opportunity to get to know Prime Minister Suhrwardy, and we liked him. He was brilliant, with a remarkable memory. He knew everyone by name and always introduced people who didn't know each other. The big parties were held on the grounds of public buildings under shamianas, which were large colorful tents, with Persian carpets spread over the grass to stand on, so that the ladies' heels wouldn't sink into the grass. The private parties were held at the prime minister's residence. Typically there was swimming, with drinks offered at the side of the large pool, followed by cocktails and dinner in black tie. The residence was huge, with a ten-foot wall surrounding the grounds. It was formerly the British governor's mansion. The parties were a good vehicle for me, enabling me to meet important people. The PM liked Americans, particularly good-looking American women, to grace his parties. His wife had died and he seemed lonely. His daughter, Begum Sulaiman, served as his official hostess. His behavior was always correct, and we were sorry that we had initially misinterpreted it.

He liked to tease. When the PM attended a party, no one was supposed to leave before he did. The problem was that he seemingly required little sleep and liked to stay up until three or four in the morning. One night we decided to sneak out through the kitchen and he spotted us. He said, "You can't leave before I do." I said, "I'm sorry, Mr. Prime Minister, but I can't stay up as late as you can."

Later on we invited him to a party at our house. As a major, I didn't expect him to come, but he did, in his limousine, with motorcycle escort, flags flying and sirens wailing. The servants couldn't believe it.

Our home was located in a new section of Karachi in an area of larger homes. The house was surrounded by a wall. There were two wrought-iron gates with a circular driveway in front of the house. Along the front of the house was a covered veranda with a terrazzo floor and columns. We had a large living room and dining room, three bedrooms and three baths. In the rear of the house there was a garage and servants quarters where the bearer, or butler, Aslam, and his helper, Hamal, lived. The ayah, or nanny, stayed in the bedroom with our two daughters. The other servants lived away from the compound. They included the cook, the gardener, the night watchman, the outside sweeper, the laundress and the seamstress. The caste system was strict and none of the servants would perform another's tasks.

A few problems arose while we were there. Hamal, who washed the dishes, let them accumulate. After washing them one day, he was carrying the dishes in a large tub from the kitchen to the pantry and dropped it, breaking all the dishes that we used on a daily basis. Replacements had to come from the United States. On another day he plugged in the vacuum cleaner using two extension cords and forgetting to use the transformer. The whole thing blew. At the time I considered homicide but didn't want to pay the penalty. After sweeping the interior of the house, he would leave the screen door open while he swept everything out to the back terrace. The flies would come in, and if there was a breeze, the dust would blow back in. He meant well but had difficulties. He wasn't the only goof-up, however. I plugged the 45rpm record player into the electric receptacle, which was 220 volts without a transformer, having not stopped to think. I left the room, and when I returned flames were shooting up from the record player, which was playing "I Don't Want to Set the World on Fire!"

After working each day from 7:00 A.M. until about 2:00 or 3.00 P.M. I would go home for lunch. When I arrived, I had to get out of the car to open the gate. This annoyed me, so I spoke to Aslam telling him that when I got home, with eight to ten servants present, I expected someone to open the gate. Aslam said that the gardener was on a siesta at that time and the night watchman wasn't on duty. "Well, then leave the gate open," I said. He responded that if he left the gate open, goats and beggars would come in. By that time I was more than annoyed. I told Aslam, "There are enough servants here, and I don't care who opens it, but when I come home someone had better be at the gate!" There was no further problem with the gate.

We made the mistake of buying a puppy for the children. The dog did what dogs do, and Memsahib (Joanne) asked Aslam to clean it up. He responded that he didn't clean up after dogs. He couldn't do that and then serve food. Well, then, let Hamal do it. He couldn't do it either. It was the job of the outside sweeper, who was only on premises for about one hour a day. That was not satisfactory. Joanne called me in tears. I called a Pakistani friend, who said that Muslims considered dogs unclean and that the best thing to do was to give the dog away.

The outsider sweepers were the low men on the totem pole. Many of them were from the class known as untouchables. Some of these unfortunates converted to Christianity to improve their lot. Some Muslims thus equated Christians with untouchables. So that no one lose face we dispensed with the dog.

The cook's position was the real problem. We had four of them in two years. They were unreliable. One of the cooks was excellent, and he could make elaborate desserts out of spun sugar that were incredibly artistic. We found that food was disappearing rapidly, however: He was taking it from the "go-down" (pantry) and selling it at the market. He had to go.

We flew the attaché plane once a month to the U.S. air base at Dharan, Saudi Arabia, to purchase food from the commissary for attaché, and State Department personnel, as there was no adequate source in Karachi. Meat was butchered and then placed on an open cart to circulate in the residential neighborhoods and to sell from the cart, which was always covered by flies. We had a refrigerator and a freezer that was shipped from the United States.

Joanne thought that if she employed someone who was untrained as a cook and trained him, he would be more loyal. She spent days in the kitchen with the next cook. He was learning, and on Thanksgiving we had the air attaché and his wife as dinner guests. When I started to carve the turkey, I pierced it with the carving fork and blood spurted up about six inches. Tinkie almost choked trying to avoid laughing. The cook had also left the plastic bag with the liver, and giblets inside the turkey. With aplomb, I carved some pieces from the outside and served them. When the pumpkin pie was served, it was frozen. Joanne had told him to bake the pie before Thanksgiving and then freeze it. So he did. Finally he became a competent cook, but then he quit, saying now that he could cook, he could get a higher paying job working for oil company personnel.

Two of the parties we gave turned out rather badly. We had decided to have an informal American party and to serve hamburgers. Aslam and the cook were instructed to grill the hamburgers. Unfortunately they decided to use kerosene to start the fire; the odor of kerosene permeated the hamburgers, and they were terrible. Additionally some of the Muslims would not eat them because of the "ham" in the name, thinking they were ham, which most Muslims do not eat.

Another evening we decided to serve Mexican food. We had a guest list of forty people. About two days before the party, the cook quit. Joanne and I had to go into the kitchen for two days to prepare the food. The kitchen was just four walls with a sink installed, and no cabinets or counters. It was primitive. Somehow we muddled through but it wasn't much fun. The party, however, was great.

Periodically we flew the attaché plane to visit various air bases around the country. Primarily we visited Lahore and Rawalpindi, two of the larger cities and more important areas. It was always enjoyable to meet the Pakistani Air Force officers at their home bases and to eat at the officers' mess.

Occasionally we had to fly the ambassador or other U.S. dignitaries to bases in East or West Pakistan, or to India or Afghanistan. Navigational aids in the area were limited, weather could be treacherous, and there were mountains to navigate over or around.

Henry Cabot Lodge while on an official visit to Pakistan requested a flight to Kabul and was dropped off there. He then asked that we return to pick him up. The weather was terrible, with limited visibility and icing conditions. We made it to Kabul with difficulty, only to find that he had decided to exit via automobile through the Khyber Pass. It was several days before weather conditions were adequate for us to return to Karachi.

The plane had to be flown to Dharan for periodic maintenance, where the USAF had facilities. On occasion, the USAF issued tech orders requiring compliance. The Air Force found intergranular corrosion in the wing bolts of C-47s and we had to make the flight 1000 miles across water to Dharan to have them checked! As pilot, I kept waiting for the wings to fall off during the flight, but they didn't. In addition, the plane had to be flown to Milan, Italy, twice a year for inspection, which took a month. The plane had seats for seven passengers, and if there was space available wives could travel. The assistant attachés took turns making the flight. It was great when you had the opportunity to go to Europe for a month, but very difficult when you were left on station for a month by yourself.

In December 1956 I wrote, "Last Monday, the 26th of November, I flew to Dharan, where we took our plane for a 100-hour inspection. We were there four days during which time I went to the PX, Commissary, played bridge and saw movies. We came back on Thursday. The trip was very pleasant both ways with beautiful weather and visibility of over 100 miles! That's better than it is in Texas. The flight is over

1000 miles each way, most of it over water; however, a good part of the flight is along the coast of Pakistan and Iran. We fly from Karachi to Jiwani to Sharjah to Dharan and return.

"Upon our return we (Lt. Col. Workman and I) learned that we were to leave the next day for New Delhi, to fly Senator Cooper who was on his way to confer with PM Nehru, as the personal representative of President Eisenhower. As you can imagine, Friday morning was very hectic: we had to get visas, clearance, money, clothes, etc. and be ready to go when Senator Cooper arrived, which was 1250. We didn't quite make it, but we did drive 12 miles to Mauripur, where we keep the plane, file clearance and fly to Karachi Civil in 35 minutes. Bryant started the engines and taxied out while I cleared and climbed aboard en route. We were just about one hour late, but the Senator wasn't ready anyway. His visa wasn't ready. Mrs. Cooper, and Senator and Mrs Javitts were in the party. We got them to Delhi about 1830, and they were met by VIPs, newspapermen, motion picture photographers, spotlights, etc. We were the forgotten men, of course, but the Air Attaché and his wife met us and took us to their house for dinner and to spend the night. Mrs. Ramsey, our hostess, is from Big Springs, Texas, and probably gave Texas its name for hospitality. Saturday morning she took us shopping and I bought a 36" brass tray, which Joanne has been wanting, to make into a coffee table. I've never seen anything like them in the States. When we get back and have to polish it, we'll probably wish we had never seen one. We got back Saturday evening. Sunday the three biggest members of the family attended church. Christy couldn't find her money when the collection plate was passed, and she was so hurt that when the service was over she started to cry. So I told the minister and he brought out the plate just for her and she was happy again.

"Monday morning Col. True and Col. Workman, Mrs. True, Mrs. Workman, Memsahib (Joanne) and crew took off on their tour of the Near East. They left for Delhi, Dacca, Rangoon, Bankok, Calcutta, Agra and Karachi. We are required to visit East Pakistan, which is on the other side of India (which presents many problems for Pakistan) on occasion. This trip was slightly extended.

"This mass exodus from Karachi left me holding the bag in more ways than one. With the other two officers gone, I am acting air attaché, which means nothing except that I'm the only one here to do the work. Since two of us were out all last week things were piled up and add to this the visit of two Four Star Generals next week, for which many things must be planned. I will have to meet their planes, etc. Then of course I am also Chief Baby Sitter and House Manager while Memsahib is gone. That involves trying to keep eight servants from goofing up things completely, such as blowing out transformers, fuses, plugs, and failing to pump water into the tank so that when you turn on the shower there 'ain't none'. Well you get the idea.

"Joanne will be gone ten to twelve days. Except for an excursion to Dharan, this is the first time she has gone out on her own. Of course she has plenty of company. We would like to be able to take some trips together but can't see leaving the children with the servants.

"The social events continue on their merry way. When I am out of town, Joanne can decline to attend parties if she so desires, but it doesn't work in reverse. It's always hello or farewell or Army day or something. Still I must admit that we enjoy the majority of the parties and haven't yet adopted the attitude of some of our 'veddy' bored with it all counterparts."

Some of the Pakistani Air Force officers became good friends and would often drop by the house. They were excellent pilots, intelligent and cultured. They were the cream of the crop. Many of them were excellent tennis and squash players, and superb at bridge. The deputy director of civil aviation and Begum Hayat became good friends as well as the Akrams. Akram had made about 25 million dollars buying surplus equipment in Burma after the war, especially C-47s which were then sold to Middle Eastern countries. The Akrams had a beautiful home designed by an Italian architect, with huge rooms, marble floors and a magnificent marble stairway that went to a landing and then curved upward both to right and left to the second floor.

The Akrams entertained beautifully. Their dining room table was Italian marble with inlaid silver. Begum Akram had magnificent jewelry, emerald, diamond, ruby and saphire necklaces, huge stones, and matching rings and bracelets. Akram died of a heart attack at age 42 shortly before we left Karachi. His death was quite unexpected and it was a very sad event.

The son and daughter and son-in-law of Malik Feroz Khan Noon, the Pakistan minister to the U.N. and then foreign minister also became friends. Noon's son-in-law, Hamid, was captain of the president's body guards, very dashing, and an excellent horseman. His son, Nur, liked cars and would often come by our house to discuss cars and life in America with me.

While Prime Minister Suhrwardy was on a visit to the United States, he unexpectedly was voted out of office, and Malik Feroz Khan Noon became prime minister of Pakistan. Before we left Karachi, Prime Minister Noon and his wife gave a seated lunch for us at his residence, inviting only my successor and the Pakistan Army chief of staff, General Haji, and their wives.

Our two-year tour in Karachi was like a scene from the *Arabian Nights*. We thoroughly enjoyed being there and liked the Pakistanis immensely. We returned on the *SS Asia* to Naples, Italy, and on the *Constitution* from Naples to New York. When we embarked in Karachi, the servants came to see us off and Chris cried because Aslam couldn't come with us. We felt the same way she did but didn't cry.

The Voyage Home

As attachés we were allowed to travel first class, but it was modified first class. Our cabin on the *SS Asia* was more nearly third-class, but we had first-class privileges. The food was marvelous and the service was excellent. We were exhausted from the preparations for moving and the many farewell parties and enjoyed the opportunity to unwind and relax.

The *Constitution* was a larger ship with more activities. After two years of not having salads available while in Pakistan, we ate all salads in sight in quantity. The food was excellent, and it was served five times a day — breakfast, lunch, dinner, tea and midnight buffet. The children shared a cabin with us but they had to eat at separate sittings. Joanne and I took turns going with them to the dining room. During the voyage they both became ill, and then Joanne contracted whatever they had, which made life difficult. Nevertheless, I loved being on board ship and had a good time.

Our cat, Lady Macbeth, was in separate quarters, with the rest of the pets. Several times after visiting the pet quarters we took the cat to our cabin for a short stay. On her first visit, upon seeing herself in the full-length mirror, she arched her back, hair standing on end, and hissed at the other cat. After deciding that the other cat wasn't a threat, she ignored it. One day the steward saw the cat in our cabin and advised that such visits were not allowed, which ended them.

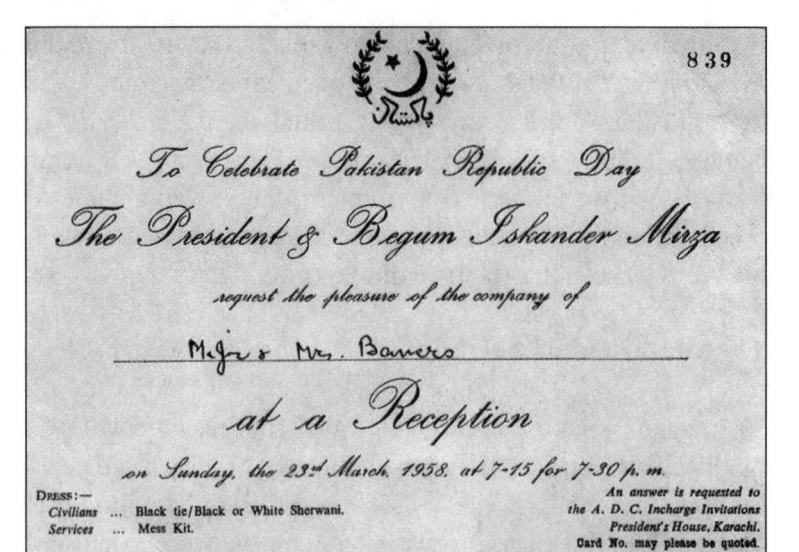

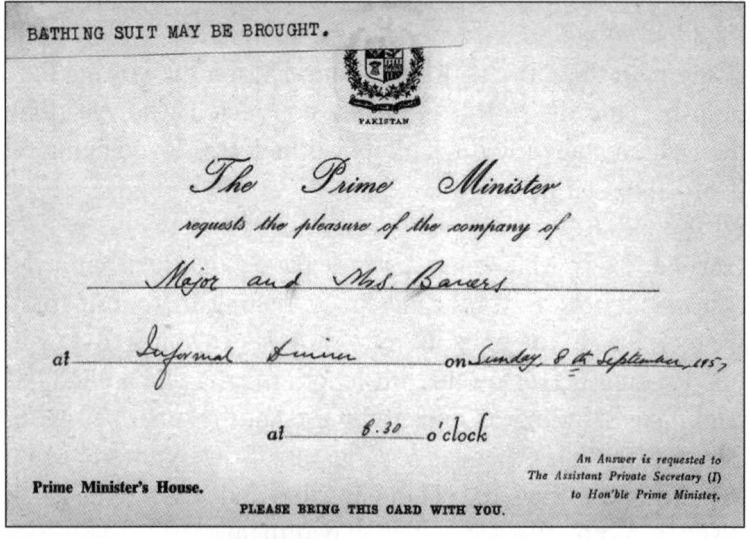

> 839
>
> To Celebrate Pakistan Republic Day
>
> The President & Begum Iskander Mirza
>
> request the pleasure of the company of
>
> _Major & Mrs. Bavers_
>
> at a Reception
>
> on Sunday, the 23rd March, 1958, at 7-15 for 7-30 p. m.
>
> Dress :—
> Civilians ... Black tie/Black or White Sherwani.
> Services ... Mess Kit.
>
> An answer is requested to the A. D. C. Incharge Invitations President's House, Karachi. Card No. may please be quoted.

> BATHING SUIT MAY BE BROUGHT.
>
> PAKISTAN
>
> The Prime Minister
>
> requests the pleasure of the company of
>
> _Major and Mrs. Bavers_
>
> at _Informal Dinner_ on _Sunday, 8th September 1957_
>
> at _8.30_ o'clock
>
> Prime Minister's House.
> PLEASE BRING THIS CARD WITH YOU.
>
> An Answer is requested to The Assistant Private Secretary (I) to Hon'ble Prime Minister.

Some of the invitations received.

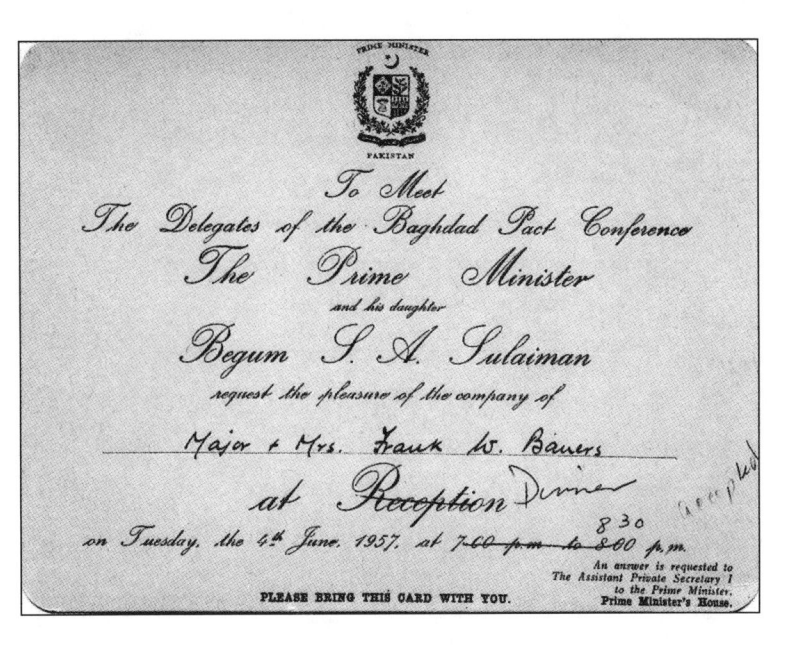

To Meet
The Delegates of the Baghdad Pact Conference
The Prime Minister
and his daughter
Begum S. A. Sulaiman
request the pleasure of the company of

Major & Mrs. Frank W. Bauers

at Reception ~~Dinner~~

on Tuesday, the 4th June, 1957, at ~~7-00 p.m.~~ to 8:00 8-30 p.m.

Accepted

PLEASE BRING THIS CARD WITH YOU.

An answer is requested to
The Assistant Private Secretary I
to the Prime Minister,
Prime Minister's House.

To Meet His Excellency Mr. Svetozar Vukmanovic
Vice President of the Federal Executive Council of the
Federal People's Republic of Yugoslavia
The Prime Minister
requests the pleasure of the company of

Major & Mrs. Frank W. Bauers

at Dinner

on Thursday, the 10th October, 1957, at 8-30 p.m.

DRESS:—
Civilians ... Black tie or Sherwani.
Services ... Mess Kit.
Prime Minister's House.

PLEASE BRING THIS CARD WITH YOU.

An Answer is requested to
The Assistant Private Secretary I
to the Prime Minister.

Mr. H. S. Suhrawardy will be delighted if you and your esteemed husband will do him the honour of spending an evening with him and friends (d. d & d) from 20-15 o'clock onwards on ___Monday___ the ___31ˢᵗ March 1958___

Informal

R.S.V.P.
Pour Memoire.

Latham House
94, Clifton,
Phone 5747. 40116

On the occasion of Battle of Britain Day
The Air Adviser to the United Kingdom High Commissioner
and
Mrs P. P. W. Sands
request the pleasure of the company of
___Major and Mrs. Frank W. Bauers, Jr.___
at a Reception
on Saturday 15th September, 1956
from 7 p.m. to 8-45 p.m.
at 230/A, Somerset Street

accepted

R.S.V.P.
U.K. High Commission

Regrets

On the occasion of the Fortieth
Anniversary of the Soviet Army and Navy
The Military, Naval and Air Attache of the USSR Embassy
Colonel V. N. Dubrovin
requests the pleasure of the company of
Major & Mrs Frank W. Bauers
at a Reception,
on Saturday 22nd of February, 1958 at 7 p. m.
at the Soviet Embassy.

R. S. V. P.
Bleak House Road No. 8/28.
Telephone: No. 52853

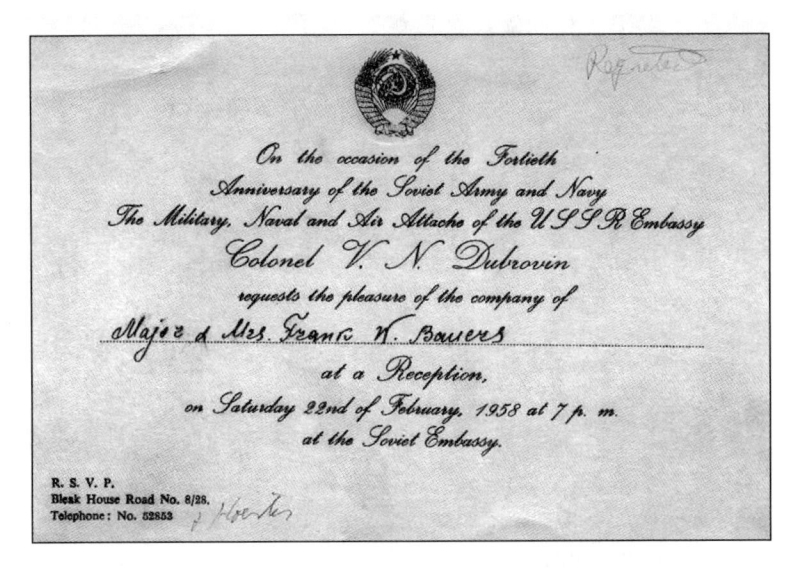

Programme

—

A Review on Change of Command

of the

Pakistan Air Force

23rd July, 1957

at

P. A. F. Mauripur

A party at our home.

Mrs. Stevenson, the host, wife of a Pan-Am pilot, Capt. Hamid Noon

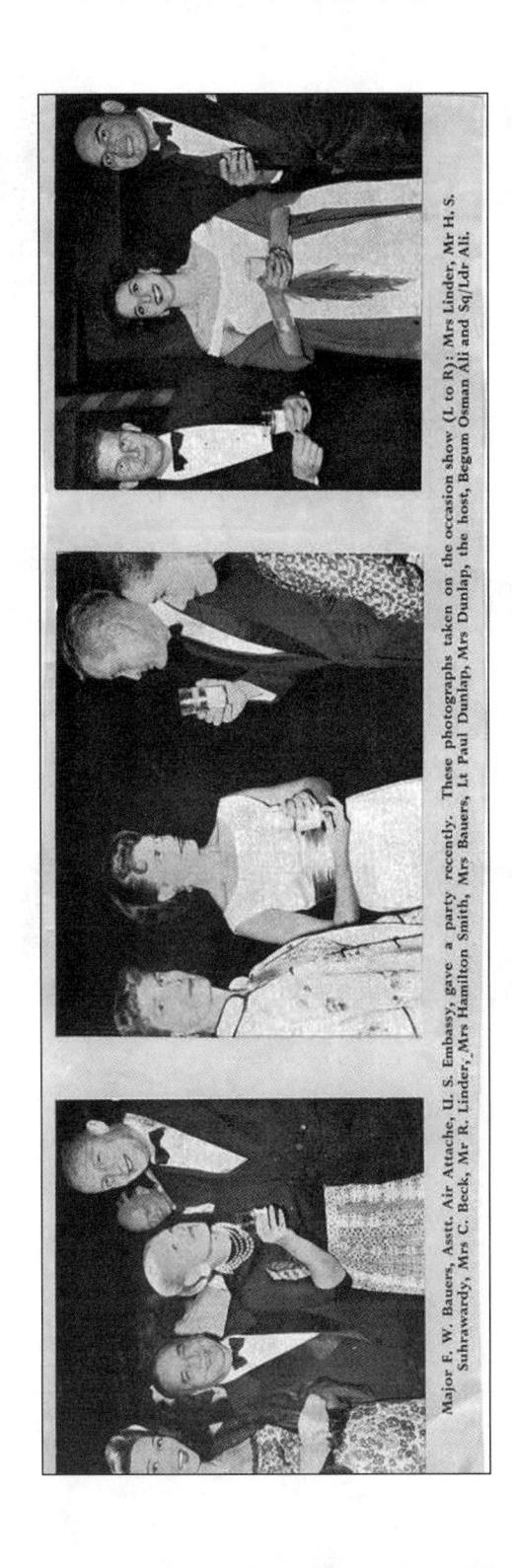

Major F. W. Bauers, Asstt. Air Attache, U. S. Embassy, gave a party recently. These photographs taken on the occasion show (L to R): Mrs Linder, Mr H. S. Suhrawardy, Mrs C. Beck, Mr R. Linder, Mrs Hamilton Smith, Mrs Bauers, Lt Paul Dunlap, Mrs Dunlap, the host, Begum Osman Ali and Sq/Ldr Ali.

Major General Louis Truman, Begum Ansari, Begum Hadid, host

Mrs. True, Colonel True, Assistant Air Attaché Designate and Mrs. Bauers, hostess Mrs. Reid

Our house in Karachi

Hamal; the cook; Aslam, the bearer; Lilly, the ayah

Joni and Christy, Valentine's Day in Karachi

CHAPTER FOURTEEN

AT THE STRATEGIC INTELLIGENCE SCHOOL

Another View of the Statue of Liberty

The *Constitution* docked in the summer of 1958 in New York City where we were met by Joanne's aunt and uncle, Jane and Bob Hills. They were driving our new 1958 Cadillac sedan which we had ordered from GM before leaving Karachi, using our diplomatic discount. Jane and Bob were kind enough to pick up the car and bring it to the dock. With our luggage, two children and the Siamese cat we went ashore. Having been advised by friends that the cat would have to go into quarantine on arrival in the States, we were surprised when the purser announced over the speaker system that we could pick up the cat and take it ashore. I didn't ask any questions. Later when I looked at the papers, I noted the release of one cat, "belonging to Lady MacBeth." Apparently believing that the cat belonged to a British aristocrat, the ship's officers deemed it undesirable to hold the cat in quarantine.

Back in the U.S.A.

Our one footlocker had been placed in the ship's hold during the voyage, so I handed the claim ticket to one of the baggage handlers and asked if he would retrieve it for us. His response was, "Get it yourself!" I said, "Well, I see that we're back in the U.S." After two years of being catered to, we were on our own, without diplomatic status, servants, allowances or assistants.

Jane and Bob took us to their apartment on Park Avenue for lunch. The butler greeted us and served lunch. It was a very delightful interlude before embarking on our trip. Jane was an interior designer who had exquisite taste and a beautiful collection of French antiques, china and silver. (A fifteenth-century chest and other pieces had been on loan to the Metropolitan Museum.) She was also a graceful and charming hostess. Jane was from a well-to-do St. Louis family, where she made her debut at the Veiled Prophet Ball. After an unhappy first marriage, Jane was divorced. When she married Bob, who was also divorced, Jane was excommunicated by the Roman Catholic Church, which caused her a great deal of distress.

Bob was in management counsel, working with major corporations. Between the two of them, Jane and Bob knew almost everyone in the United States worth knowing and were a great team both socially and in business.

After lunch with Jane and Bob Hills we drove to Swarthmore, Pennsylvania, where we spent the night with Joanne's Aunt Alice and Uncle Bill. Their English-country stone house seemed huge to us after our three-week ocean trip with four of us in one cabin. Aunt Alice asked what sleeping arrangements we preferred, and we said we would all like separate rooms. "My, what a close-knit family, " she remarked. We had an excellent dinner and, exhausted, slept very well.

The next day we headed south to Washington, D.C. and Falls Church in Northern Virginia, where Joanne's mother, whom we called Mama, lived. She had visited us in Karachi about mid-tour and had had a great time. After a visit with Mama, we continued south to San Antonio. Lady MacBeth, did not like riding in the car and would get up on the dashboard in front of me, blocking my vision and creating a major distraction. I was nervous anyway driving a new car, on the right side of the road, after two years of driving on the left side in Pakistan, and we were in unfamiliar territory with two kids and a Siamese cat. So the cat soon found herself staying in a kitty kennel for a few weeks while we drove to Texas and back.

My parents were happy to see us and to see the children after our two-year sojourn on the other side of the world. We had a good visit, and I liked being back in San Antonio and having a few Tex-Mex meals at La Fonda's, my favorite Mexican restaurant. Soon it was necessary to return to Washington, where I was assigned to the Strategic Intelligence School (SIS) as an instructor.

Habitat Northern Virginia

We looked at houses for sale in Washington and Northern Virginia but decided to rent rather than buy after our experience of being unable to sell the house in Wayne. In the military service you often have to sell when transferred rather than at an appropriate time. A house around the corner from Mama's was available for lease, and we leased it. The location was very convenient for baby-sitting. When we wanted to go out for the evening, we could drop the kids off at Mama's and let them spend the night. All concerned liked the arrangement.

Another factor was favorable: Mama worked at the Main Navy Building, where SIS was located, so we could carpool most of the time, and she liked to drive. I bought a 1951 Ford two-door from the Navy commander across the street and it made an excellent second car, with a lot of pep. With snow tires and chains it could go almost anywhere, and it was fun to drive. I drove the Ford to Washington when I had school at night, and to Bolling or Andrews when I was going to fly.

The School at Main Navy (SIS)

The Main Navy Building actually was a series of buildings built on the Mall between the Washington and Lincoln Monuments during the war. They were frame buildings, and I rather liked them except for the rats one could encounter in the halls at night. These were *Large* rats. Fortunately I didn't work at night too often. These buildings were later torn down, and the Vietnam Memorial is located on the site.

The General Instruction Department had the responsibility for planning the curriculum for the Attaché Course and the Intelligence Course, setting up the schedules, obtaining guest lecturers and assigning staff lecturers, conducting examinations and grading them. We met the lecturers, introduced them to the class, and critiqued them. For guest speakers we were able to draw from the top levels of Defense, CIA, the State Department and other agencies and from the universities in the Washington area.

My basic responsibility was the Attaché Course. Having just returned from attaché duty I was selected to teach as I was considered to have the required knowledge to instruct those who were going out. During my tour of duty, for a period of about six months, I also was acting chief of the general instruction department, GID, which was a position that I liked very much. The position called for an Army colonel and I was an Air Force major, therefore I didn't get to keep it. The colonel who was assigned to fill the spot was totally out of his element, so I had to continue to handle much of the responsibility for the department and many of the chief's duties. He tended to take credit for anything that went well, and blame anything that didn't go well either on me or on Major Doering, the WAC officer who worked with me. The colonel had trouble keeping things straight. He had served, in my opinion, too much combat duty. The Air Force would have called him flak-happy.

A Matter of Introduction

One day the deputy director of the CIA was scheduled to speak. The colonel decided that he wanted to introduce this speaker. Anne Marie and I briefed him on the man, his position, his importance, and the subject that he would address.

On his arrival, we conducted the deputy director to the colonel's desk and introduced him. After a minute or so of small talk, the colonel inquired, "Oh, by the way, what agency are you with?" Anne Marie and I wanted to crawl under our desks.

Major Doering, WAC

Anne Marie was intellectual, very well educated and fluent in four languages. She had lived and gone to school in French Indochina, where her father was with a major oil company. She was very valuable to the Army during the Vietnam war, speaking the Annamese language as well as French, and being knowledgeable about the country. Anne Marie and I worked well together and got along well. She was an asset to the department and to the school. We usually had lunch together because we could discuss our work at the school as well as many other topics. There was gossip at the school, however, which offended and annoyed me, and we had to desist. I had thought the country was beyond that.

SIS and Fort Holabird

The Strategic Intelligence School was under the command of Fort Holabird, in Maryland. The commander of Fort Holabird also held the title of Commandant of SIS, while the colonel who was in charge of the school was designated as assistant commandant. Before leaving the school, I wrote a staff study recommending that this arrangement be changed because it was awkward and affected relationships with other agencies. It was unfair to the officer who was running the school and served no valid purpose. I never heard what the reaction was to my study.

The General's Visit

The assistant commandant and the chief of the GID seemed fearful of anyone saying or doing the wrong thing when a senior officer visited the school. At one point a general was scheduled for a visit, and there was a flurry of activity in preparation and some trepidation. We were not told the general's name, but Anne Marie and I had been briefed several times as to what to do and what to say. The big day arrived, and we were summoned to the assistant commandant's office to meet the general. I walked in and the general said, "Hi, Bill," and I responded, "Hi, Bob." Both colonels almost flipped out! It happened that the general and I had been taking a night class together at GWU for several months and were on a first-name basis. The moment was priceless.

The Chief, GID

The chief of the GID was a combat officer, a paratrooper who didn't fit in at SIS. When he left SIS to return to troop duty he was killed in a jump, when both his main chute and reserve chute failed to open — a most unusual occurrence, and most unfortunate.

I was very grateful to him for the effectiveness report that he gave me and for discussing it with me. Both the Army and the Air Force required officers to rate officers subordinate to them periodically and upon change of assignment. The colonel told me that though he did not like me personally, he did not let that affect his rating. He thought that my job performance merited an outstanding rating, which he gave me along with very favorable comments. I'm sure that it helped me to gain my promotion to lieutenant colonel while I was at SIS.

The Instructor

As a lieutenant in the Army I had instructed troops and conducted basic training, but it had been a while. Being the instructor in a classroom with a group of senior officers as students was also a bit different. Nevertheless I got into the swing of it and really liked introducing speakers to the joint classes and teaching prospective attachés. I spent the necessary time to learn the background of the speakers and to prepare the introduction and the hours necessary to prepare lesson plans, worksheets, practical exercises and examinations. I felt confident because of my success in Pakistan and the favorable comments that both the Embassy and the Attaché office received from the State Department and from Air Force Intelligence.

The Attaché Course was six months long so I got to know a number of officers while I was instructing. A few became friends, but generally the relationships were formal. Some of the students didn't want to be there, some thought the school was a waste of time, most were noncommittal, and a few were very eager to learn. A few of the senior colonels believed that they had nothing to learn, and they could be difficult. Adults who become students often seem to revert to adolescence, fail to do their homework, act up in class, and try to ruffle the instructor. For the most part I was respectful. On the other hand, I didn't put up with anything. The course was important and the majority wanted to learn. The few could not be allowed to prevent their learning.

Pursuing a Master's Degree

When we returned to Washington, D.C., I was determined to take advantage of the educational opportunity and go back to George Washington University to pursue a master's degree in business administration, an M.B.A. at night. Graduate work was stimulating. Most of the classes were seminars rather than lectures, as in undergraduate work, and papers were usually required for each course. I preferred this approach to learning. I also liked the grading system: unsatisfactory, satisfactory and excellent. The only difficulties that I had were going to class after working all day and trying to write or study at home with two small children in the next room. The most difficult part was writing the required thesis. It took me three months to get approval for the topic, which was "The Application of Intelligence to Business and the Decision Making Process," and months to write the thesis The subject was hot but just a few years ahead of its time. The thesis led to my first job after leaving the military service.

I managed to achieve an "excellent" rating in all but two courses. In one course the professor had my name confused with that of another student. During the entire course he would call each of us by the other's name. He admitted the confusion and the mistake when I approached him, but he didn't change my grade. The final exam for the other satisfactory course was given the night before my departure for Texas to see my father, who was having an operation for perforated ulcers. I was concerned about the operation and about waiting to leave for Texas.

Farewell

Pop died that night, the night of the final. I had debated whether to fly to Texas sooner, but wanted to finish my course work and examinations. I thought it would be better to visit after the operation. The surgeon, however, had stopped the anticoagulants that Pop had been taking, and he died of a coronary thrombosis prior to the operation.

We had visited Texas the summer before, and I have a feeling Pop knew that it was the last time he would see us. For the first time he had tears in his eyes when we left. It is difficult to face the death of a parent: it is as though your worst fear has been realized. As a child, after attending several funerals, I was afraid that my parents might die. For years as a child you are dependent for sustenance and, after being on your own, for advice and support in your endeavors. Then in an instant your source of advice and encouragement is gone and it is difficult to adjust.

Assisting the Executor

I spent a week in Texas assisting my mother with the many things that needed to be done and with the administration of the estate. She was emotionally devastated and didn't know what her financial situation would be. Fortunately I was able to assist in Washington by meeting with personnel of the Army Mutual Aid Association, which provided tremendous help with insurance and benefits. The problems were resolved, and Mother had the house and a comfortable income for the rest of her life.

Flying Time

One of the difficulties for an Air Force pilot assigned to a desk job was getting time off to fly and then taking the barbs from the nonrated Air Force and Army officers concerning time away and flight pay. In a school situation it was particularly bad because of class schedules. It wasn't possible to just take off. Thus any flying I did had to be at night or on a weekend. My total schedule of commuting, working, flying, attending class, writing papers and studying left no time for either my family or myself. After attaché duty in Karachi, it was difficult to adjust to the Washington situation, especially for Joanne. She threatened to burn my desk when I finished graduate school, and I felt that I might burn it before she did.

My efforts to earn a bachelors degree were worthwhile in that I succeeded, but rather than help my advancement in the Air Force, I believe that hindered it. For two years in school I was out of circulation. As a result of my education I was assigned to the Air Force Auditor General, which I liked, but it took me out of the mainstream of flying and command. The attaché assignment was the only way out of the Auditor General, and it was "way out", in terms of both the Air Force and the location. While an attache assignment had prestige it was not helpful for advancement. The assignment to an Army School in the Main Navy Building was the final nail.

In the fifteen years following WWII, the Air Force had advanced to jet aircraft, and I was still flying prop jobs on a part-time basis. Seven times I had applied for jet transition training, and seven times my application had been rejected.

Congress was placing pressure on the Air Force to reduce expenditures by removing officers whose current jobs did not require flying from flight status. I disagreed with the applicability of that point, in that the attaché position required flight status and I was instructing attachés who were going on assignment. Nevertheless, the Air Force issued a list of officers who were selected for removal from flight status, and my name was on it. At that point I walked into the assistant commandant's office and advised him of my intent to leave the service. He and other staff officers offered to appeal the grounding and to assist in any way. They were able to get me assigned to jet transition at Randolph AFB.

Within a short time the Air Force rescinded the grounding order because of the large number of pilots resigning or requesting retirement. The rescission order was as offensive to me as the original order, if not more so. My thought was that either the initial grounding wasn't essential or there was a lack of resolve in meeting the situation that initiated it. Our lives were in disarray for months. We were barely surviving financially in Washington with flight pay and didn't feel that we could survive without it. Thinking about the decision, at age 39, I felt it was too late for jet transition. I had made my decision to leave the service, and I decided that I wasn't going to change it.

Following the Sign to the Exit

There were valid reasons for me to exit the service. While trying to improve my qualifications, I wound up away from what I had originally wanted: assignment to an air base with a flying unit. I started out well but hadn't attempted to control my assignments; I failed to attach myself to someone who was going places, although I had the opportunities to do so. I didn't think that was the way I wanted to go. There was the problem of the "hump," which basically was a problem of too many officers in the same age group and grade.

The type of flying that I was doing was dangerous because we didn't get enough flying time to maintain proficiency as a pilot or to keep up with instrument procedures. Witness the deaths of many of my friends. A successor at SIS also was killed shortly after taking over the job. Finally, there was the matter of income, which was marginal, and the numerous transfers we had had in ten years. The moves were expensive and disruptive.

On the other side of the coin, I felt that I was young enough to pursue another career. Bob Hills had asked me to get out of the Air Force and come to work with him in New York in an exciting new venture with considerably more income. So as much as I liked the service, the time had come to leave it. I felt that the service wasn't the same after WWII as it had been before, and I was ready to move on, with appreciation for what I had had in the service and enthusiasm for a new endeavor.

Thoughts About Military Service

Military life was challenging, and I gained much from it: an education, many great experiences, wonderful friendships, exciting travel and new skills. The organization and discipline of the military system, the sense of purpose and service to the country were and are appealing to me. There were as in all avenues of life, some disadvantages, but they were of little importance. Military service should not be avoided; it is rewarding in many ways, and it is imperative that this country maintain a strong defense.

In the service one can have great responsibilities at an early age and an opportunity to work in many different capacities, generating confidence in one's ability to handle almost any situation or new position. It is possible to specialize, which these days may be essential. During my career I was a platoon leader, a pilot, an auditor, a diplomat, an intelligence officer, operations officer, personnel director, and an executive and manager, enabling development of useful skills.

The Air Force years were memorable, and the B-26 was a great aircraft, though I learned to associate flying with being shot at. I remember Johnny Eckert, Bill Geary, Johnny Catlin, Bill Ottinger, Ricky Carter and others as irreplaceable friends, and I salute them. There have been many players on the stage, and they have had "their exits and their entrances."

Retirement: A Change in Focus

My request for retirement after 20 years of service, seventeen years with the Air Force, had to be submitted to the secretary of the Air Force for approval. It was approved. I was asked if I wanted a retirement ceremony and my response was " No, just a certificate of service."

In a way it seemed ironic to be leaving the service. The service life was what I had always wanted. I had been promoted to the grade of lieutenant colonel in the regular Air Force and had the right to stay on active duty for a minimum of another eight years. I was still flying. But like many other things in life it wasn't what I had envisioned. Life on an airbase and being part of a unit was what had appealed to me. Other than in combat, I had never been assigned to a base or to a squadron. Joanne and I had lived as civilians with the disadvantages of military service and few of the advantages. I truly enjoyed most of my life in the service and have never regretted any of it. I loved the Air Force and being a pilot. On the other hand I have not regretted getting out or where it has taken us.

Two Lives

Moving to New York was exciting, and the transition was easy. From management counsel I went on to building and development and commercial and international real estate brokerage, and to writing and publishing.

Although the path taken was different from that originally planned, I am grateful for the opportunity that I had to become a pilot, to serve my country in time of war, during the Cold War and in time of peace and to make a contribution. Nothing can replace the feeling of being a member of the Air Force, the friendships or the comraderie with other pilots and crew members.

There is an another world, however, and that also has been great, meeting new challenges and making contributions in business, building subdivisions, and planning resort communities. Working in international real estate with counterparts in Spain, France and Mexico, has been immensely satisfying. Writing nonfiction is enabling me to pass on what I have found to be of value, both in business and in personal affairs.

Being a pilot was an exciting and romantic profession. As the allure began to fade, with an M.B.A. and a great job opportunity in New York City, I was eager to start a new life, with no regrets for the old and with anticipation of the new.

The constant in my life has been my beautiful wife and our love and marriage. We have built a rewarding life and have two sucessful daughters, one a computer-software engineer, the other a mental-health therapist and counselor, at present engaged as a homemaker and mother of two children. Joanne is a painter who shows in New York and has shown internationally. She prefers modern works using acrylic and mixed media. My current efforts are directed toward real estate, trust management, writing nonfiction and publishing. I have published *Where There's A Will..., A Guide for the Executor or Administrator of an Estate* and am working on a financial and estate-planning guide and other books. Throttles forward!

APPENDIX

COMBAT PILOT

First we had primary training
Flying when it wasn't raining
Upgraded to a larger plane
We joined others in the chain
Of Pilots confident and snooty
Who chose this way to do their duty

Of the country's men we were the best
Having been put to the test
Queried on algebra and grammar
Our knees hit with a hammer
Taking flights in simulation
Without other stimulation

Off to combat after a while
No longer living in style
Gone the apartment and the girl
Gone the mad party whirl
Gone the convertible - top down
Gone the glamour - man about town

And the enemy knew how to shoot!
Although we didn't give a hoot
We knew someday we would be
A part of living history
And if the flak had our name on it
Well it might become a sonnet

There was a thrill about it all
We could soar and we could fall
We could fight the war on high
And look upon the sea and sky
Away from misery and mud
And hope the bomb was not a dud

Our many friends who bought the farm
Why were they not saved from harm?
Returning to our huts at night
The empty bunks - too much to sight
We suffered the loss and placed the blame
On bad luck, collision, flak and flame

When the war at last was over
We knew we wouldn't be in clover
The folks at home, they could not know
What we had felt, and told us so
In many ways they could not see
And we were no longer young and free

War brought to us a Victory
A hero's welcome - let us be
Through the sky we cannot roam
Although it's better being at home
And yet we miss the call of old
When we were young and brave and bold

F. William Bauers, Jr.
1979

COMBAT MISSIONS FLOWN

Date	Target	Type of Target	Results
March 7, 1944	Conches	Airdrome	Exc
March 8	Soesterburg	Airdrome	Adequate
March 20	Creil	Marshalling Yard	Exc
March 23	Creil	Marshalling Yard	Exc
March 25	Hirson	Marshalling Yard	
March 26	Ijmuiden	Submarine Pens	Fair
April 10 a.m.	Le Havre	Gun Battery	Poor
p.m.	Namur	Marshalling Yard	Fair
April 12	St. Ghislain Middlekerke AF	Marshalling Yard	Fair
April 13	Le Havre	Coastal gun	No attack
April 22 a.m.	Le Plouy Ferme	Noball	Exc
p.m.	Siracourt	Noball	Fair
April 23 a.m.	Heuringhem	Noball	Exc
April 25 p.m.	Houlgate	Coastal defense	Exc
April 26	St. Ghislain	Marshalling Yard	Good
April 28	Creil	Marshalling Yard	No attack
May 1 p.m.	Douai	Marshalling Yard	Exc
May 8 p.m.	Audinstun	Construction site	Exc
May 9 a.m.	Calais	Railway facilities	Fair
May 10 a.m.	Mons	Marshalling Yard	Exc
May 24 p.m.	Denain Ploury	Airdrome	Good
May 25	Lille Nord	Airdrome	No attack
May 27 p.m.	Nantes Gassicourt	RR Bridge	Exc
May 28 a.m.	Paris	RR Bridge	No attack
May 28 p.m	Amiens	Marshalling Yard	Fair
May 30	Rouen	Highway Bridge	Good
June 4	Courcelles-Sur Seine	Bridge	Exc
June 5	Wissant	H.Q.	Fair
June 7 p.m.	Argentan	Marshalling Yard	Fair
June 13 a.m.	Domfront	Marshalling Yard	No attack

231

June 14 p.m.	Quinville	O/D Battery	Exc
June 15 a.m.	Chartres	RR Bridge	Exc
June 20 am.	La Belle Hotesse	V Bomb	Fair
June 21	Autheaux	V Bomb	Pathfinder
June 24 p.m.	Beauvais	Marshalling Yard	Good
July 6	Domfront La Chappele	RR Bridge	Gross
July 7	Tours	RR Bridge	Exc
July 9	Rouen	Highway Bridge	No attack
July 16 a.m.	Ambrieres	RR Bridge	Pathfinder
July 16 p.m.	Foret de la Guerche	Fuel Dump	Area
July 19	Angens- Le Pont de Ce	RR Bridge	Exc
July 23 a.m.	Ambrieres	RRBridge	
July 25 a.m.	Maintenon	RR Bridge	Fair
July 28 p.m.	Semonches	Fuel Dump	Pathfinder
Aug 16	Foret de Roumaire	Ammo Dump	Recalled
Aug 17	Pont Audemer	Bridge	PFF
Aug 25	Brest	AA Guns	Area
Aug 27 a.m.	Rouen		No attack
Aug 27 p.m.	Foret de Samoussy	Fuel Dump	Area
Aug 28	Hamm	Fuel Dump	Exc
Sept 1	Brest	Gun Positions	Good
Sept 5	Brest	Gun Positions	Fair
Sept 11 p.m.	Metz	Fort	Fair
Sept 19	Duren	Marshalling Yard	Exc
Sept 23	Venlo	Marshalling Yard	No attack
Oct 2	Ubach	Industrial area	No bomb
Oct 7	Arnheim	Highway Bridge	Exc
Oct 29	Mayen	RR Bridge	PFF
Nov 3	Konz Karthaus	RR Bridge	PFF
Nov 11	Putzcoln	Strong points	PFF
Nov l9 am	Nuenburg	RR Bridge	Exc
Nov 19 p.m.	Nuwied	RR Bridge	No bombs

BIBLIOGRAPHY

The Martin B-26 Marauder
J.K. Havener
Southern Heritage Press, St. Petersburg, Florida, 1998

344th Bomb Group (M) "Silver Streaks"
History & Remembrances World War II
Edited by Lambert D. Austin
Southern Heritage Press, St. Petersburg, Florida, 1996

Marauder Men
John O. Moench, Major General USAF (Ret)
Malia Enterprises, Inc., Longwood, Florida, 1999

Flak Bait
Devon Francis
Duell Sloan & Pearce, New York, 1948

The Martin Marauder B-26
Victor C. Tannehill
Boomerang Publishers, Arvada, colorado, 1997

Wings of Courage
Jack D. Stovall, Jr.
Global Press, Memphis, Tennessee, 1991

Europe
The Illustrated Book About Europe
Felix Sutton
Grosset & Dunlap, New York, 1962

Flak Facts
**A Brief History of Flak and Flak Intelligence
In the Ninth Air Force**
Flak Section, Hq. Ninth Air Force (Adv.)

Life's Picture History of WW II
Edited by Arthur B. Tortellot
Time Inc., New York, 1950

New York Times Headlines 1900 - 1950
New York Times

To contribute to the history of the B-26 Marauder contact:

B-26 Marauder Historical Society
Post Office Box 788
Annandale, VA 22003

For information subscribe to:

The Marauder Thunder
B-26 Marauder Historical Society
Post Office Box 788
Annandale, VA 22003
or
Milk Run
344th Bomb Group Association
5747 Darnell Street
Houston, TX 77096

Submit artifacts, memorabilia, histories or documents to:

Stephanie Mitchell, Archivist
Marauder Archive
Pima Air & Space Museum
6000 E. Valencia Road
Tucson, AZ 85706